Love, Mom

A Memoir
by
Cynthia Baseman

Bloomington, IN Milton Keynes, UK
 authorHOUSE®

AuthorHouse™
1663 Liberty Drive, Suite 200
Bloomington, IN 47403
www.authorhouse.com
Phone: 1-800-839-8640

AuthorHouse™ UK Ltd.
500 Avebury Boulevard
Central Milton Keynes, MK9 2BE
www.authorhouse.co.uk
Phone: 08001974150

First published by AuthorHouse 9/5/2006

ISBN: 1-4259-5051-5 (sc)

Library of Congress Control Number: 2006906329

Printed in the United States of America
Bloomington, Indiana

This book is printed on acid-free paper.

Grateful acknowledgment is made for permission to reprint the following copyrighted material:

Page 232, Milne, A.A.. Spring Morning. Reprinted courtesy of The Trustees of the Pooh Properties included with permission of Curtis Brown Group, Ltd., London

Photograph credit: title page, Steven Ijams

For Neal

ACKNOWLEDGEMENTS

I want to thank those who helped me during my time of trouble. Forever thanks to Neal for not letting me hit the rocks; to my parents for reminding me of the good things I had in my life; to Bobby, I cannot count the number of times you lifted my heart and brought me joy; to Harrison for turning on the sun; to Greg for your compassion and wisdom; to Hayley for giving the moral support of a sister; to Julie for being a new friend who acted more like an old one; to Dr. Gail Mezrow for her support and professional eye; and to Renee Brook for being an ally. I also want to thank Gordon Kirkland for the good-natured shove to get this book to the next step and Sylvia Taylor for her editorial assistance. Finally, I owe thanks to Sunny, my canine companion, who sat by my side through endless re-writes.

AUTHOR'S NOTE

The only one I tell my secrets to is my horse.

-- Rosie Curtis, 1900

Writing a memoir is a risky venture and I had many sleepless nights wondering if the effort was at all wise. Worries took hold of me that I might experience a measure of fame or other personal gain from tragedy. Also, I feared that, by exposing the private thoughts of those closest to me, I might be inadvertently hurting or angering them.

Over time, I have met a great many women and men whose lives had been forever changed by the loss of a child. From those exchanges, I became convinced that sharing my story was the right thing to do. I have, however, changed many names, settings and descriptions so I keep secret that which ought to remain so.

The excursion is the same when you go looking for your sorrow as when you go looking for your joy.

-- Eudora Welty

Contents

PREFACE

This story grew from a series of raw journal entries and love letters to my baby, Samantha Morgan, who died without warning on May 10, 1995.

Great writing projects are like love affairs you can't wait to get back to each day. They are the last thing on your mind when you fall asleep and when you wake in the morning; you're longing to take hold of them. Clearly, writing this story wasn't one of them. My desire for the rough draft to be the final draft, to put this all behind me and move on, was not working out as planned. A decade ago I mistook a work in progress for a final draft and my manuscript drifted like a restless ghost, rattling the shelf of my black metal file cabinet, alarming as the starting bell of a boxing fight.

My fate often reminds me of the well-known boxing match the summer of 1936 when Max Schmeling struck Joe Louis's head with such ferocity it resulted in Louis's first knockdown in a professional Heavyweight Championship. While Louis won his re-match, he swore to his dying day he'd never fully recover from the punch Schmeling dealt him.

Since the moment my doctor whispered to me, "This baby is dead," I've never been able to fully recover either. How did my baby die with no warning when I had a skilled doctor caring for me?

When I took the very best care of myself possible? When I was privileged to live in one of the wealthiest cities in the richest country in the world?

Fine cracks in my marriage made me wonder: Is this a normal climate for couples that have been together for years? Is my restlessness new? Divorce among bereaved parents is common. Recent studies have found the effects of long-term grief are similar to the post-traumatic stress syndrome plaguing war veterans. Shame and guilt over losing a baby prevents many parents from seeking help. Traditional options for those that do are counseling, psychotherapy and anti-depressants. Others search for solace in support groups, on-line grief resources and volunteer opportunities.

Desperate for relief and understanding, I took a stab at just about everything. To the outside world I appeared to be getting along pretty well, but inside I remained a wreck. William Faulkner reportedly said, "Not only is the past not dead. It ain't even passed."

Accepting the reality of death might have come easier if I hadn't, up to that point, led a fairly charmed life. My husband and I had been married five years and were deeply in love. Our first baby, Bobby, was healthy and charming. Traveling was a shared passion but truthfully, we were giddy just doing the grocery shopping together.

Less than a mile away, my folks still lived in my childhood home where they'd shared a life for three decades. Down the block from them, my superstar of a brother Greg and his caring wife Hayley, had bought a home. We sought out each other's company at any celebration and during many vacations, as well.

World travel was my Dad's great love and by the time I turned twelve, my family had been to Europe, North and East Africa, Japan, even Indonesia, including New Guinea, still considered by some as one of the most dangerous destinations on earth. While I know many families bond through a shared love of team sports or an appreciation of music or any number of things, I am hard pressed to describe the kind of bond my family shares as a result of our adventures abroad.

My childhood and teenage years were happy ones; I had a great group of pals, did well in school, rode horses and played team tennis. My folks raised my brother and me with all the same freedoms and opportunities and I grew up with the notion that if I worked hard like my folks had, the sky was the limit.

Since leaving USC Cinema School I had worked for several independent producers, mostly doing research, manning phones and brewing French roast to perfection. Over time, I sold a few projects here and there. All in all, I had risen to various degrees of unsuccessful. After my first son Bobby was born, professional aspirations took a back seat to being a mom.

Before losing my baby, my existence was rather predictable and with the exception of travel, even humdrum by some standards. It seemed to me if you were a good person, the world was truly round. Loss was not something I had to deal with in any personal depth and as a result, I was horribly unequipped to handle tragedy when it came my way. I didn't deserve it, couldn't accept it, and went out of my mind trying to make sense of it.

The driving force behind this writing project was an overwhelming desire to come to terms with why I lost my daughter and to somehow reach out to her through the process. The truth is the answer didn't turn out to be straightforward. In the end, what mattered most was the journey.

CHAPTER 1:

WHEN WE WERE YOUNG

Marvin Gaye's "How Sweet It Is" blared through the speakers of the den as I sashayed up and down the room, graceful as a cow, holding hands with Bobby, my good-natured toddler. Judging by the look of the tub that was my abdomen, he was about to become a big brother any minute. But looks can be deceiving. I'd been expecting to go into labor for a week, maybe longer. Bobby and I made a sharp turn and the sweatshirt I had tied around my waist undid itself and slid down my bulging belly toward my hips. I quickly let go of my Bobby's hands and rescued the gray cotton fabric in my fingertips before it landed on the floor. Cinching the sleeves of the garment tight around my middle like a corset gave me a secure feeling, like my stomach might actually shrink back to its former life someday. Whether it was the constricting shirt, which I doubt, or the beat of the music, my unborn daughter reacted by giving me a firm kick to the top right rib. My breath caught in my throat until I readjusted myself to get the pressure off. A minute later, pop, she got me again.

I looked at Bobby. "Your sister's a big mover and shaker." The whole last trimester of the pregnancy, she ruled the late afternoons and early evenings with her own boogie routine. "Little chicken, I need a bathroom break," I said.

"Again?" Bobby raised his blond eyebrows at me.

"What can I say?" I started for the bathroom.

"Can *I* have a dance?" I heard my husband ask. I turned around and saw my husband Neal set down his briefcase and squat low with his arms outstretched. With the music on, I hadn't heard him enter the house.

"Daddeee!" Bobby yelled over the music as he ran into my husband's embrace. I reached around Neal and Bobby, aware of the baby's elbows and knees jutting within me, and gave them each a kiss. Neal snaked a hand around the place where my waist would have been and gave me a loving squeeze.

Bobby clutched Neal's hand like a train whistle and gave it a tug. "Dance, Daddy!"

"Anything?" Neal asked, as Bobby dragged him away for a dance.

"Same old. Same old. Tomorrow I have another appointment with Dr. Starre."

"Care to join our dance?"

The baby moved again, this time pressing down on my bladder. "I'll take a rain check."

The next day was Tuesday and I had a date with my husband for lunch at Il Fornaio, one of our favorite restaurants. As usual, it was packed with an international crowd and snippets of Farsi, Hebrew and Japanese echoed off the polished wood floors and tall ceilings. Despite the air-conditioning, constant sips of ice water and the menu, which I'd transformed into a fan, for the life of me, I could not cool down. My white linen maternity blouse clung to my lower back and looked wrinkled enough to have come out of the dirty laundry hamper. I tried to distract myself by looking at the harsh glint reflecting off the windshields of the passing cars. Summer had the upper hand on spring though it was only May.

Mid-week lunches with Neal were rare and I didn't want the romantic feel marred by slow service. Time was my husband's oxygen and he always seemed on the verge of gasping for more. Its scarcity was the reason, he said, for not playing eighteen holes, for not making love as often as he would like, even for holding his bladder for hours on end at the office during TV pilot season. At the first opportunity, I flagged down a waiter who took note of my protruding belly and assured me in his heavily affected Italian accent that our food would be out of the kitchen "very soon, signora."

As promised, the server promptly brought our meals out. Neal draped his colorful silk tie back over one shoulder and savored his bowl of pasta and chicken. He's an elegant man with a long face, strong jaw and kind eyes. Whether his eyes are set on the gardener or Chairman of the studio, he looks them straight in the eye, his full attention on them. He brought the pasta shells to his mouth, careful not to stain his white shirt from The Custom Shop.

His deals for the studio where he worked were spotless as well. Motivated by a fire in the belly, along with Neal's success were a few singe marks. The pressure ate at him and I winced a little as he'd come home each weeknight, biting his nails to the quick while trying to lose himself in whatever baseball game was on the television. Helpless to relieve much of the leaden feeling he carried on his

3

shoulders, I consoled myself with seeing to it Bobby was being raised right and my unborn child was getting everything she needed.

For nine months I had been getting to know my baby girl. Samantha looked delicate in her ultrasounds and felt feisty in my womb. Whereas Bobby had swayed from side to side, she punched and kicked her way around.

"Aren't I the lucky one, getting you all to myself?" I smiled across the table at Neal and he took my hand and shot me a mock-serious grin. If he wasn't meeting with other attorneys, producers, executives or agents, he saved time by grabbing lunch at his desk.

When I glanced back at Neal, he was holding up his credit card, already trying to get the waiter's attention.

"I saw Dr. Starre," I said.

"What's the story?"

"He asked how we felt about inducing labor since I'm a little dilated."

"She's only two days late. Wasn't Bobby a week late?"

"Yes. Maybe Starre's got a trip planned."

"Right. He never leaves his patients. Isn't that one of the reasons you chose him?"

"Yeah, that and the fact he delivered Julia Roberts' twins."

"Really?"

"No," I laughed. "Anyway, he thinks the baby is ready."

"What do you think?" Neal signed the credit card receipt and handed it back to the waiter.

"What difference can one more day make?" I shrugged.

"Let Mother Nature take her course."

Mother Nature. All that is wholesome and right. *Bitch* is what comes to mind these days whenever I hear the phrase.

Back at home, I let Dr. Starre know we weren't ready to induce and promised to call him the next day to advise him of any progress. By early evening, however, I began to feel sick to my stomach. I managed to prepare dinner but as soon as Neal got home, I curled up on the couch some distance from the aroma of lamb chops and steamed broccoli, which was sending my stomach into somersaults. My hand rested on my hard, round belly as if it were already cradling the baby.

Neal and Bobby finished dinner and I heard their plates clattering in the sink. Neal called over to me, "The sink's stopped up!"

"See if you can snake it out." I sat up feeling useless. The back door whined as Neal opened it and trudged down the driveway to grab the garden hose we kept near the rose bushes. When I heard his footsteps re-enter the kitchen, I called out.

"You know, honey? She's not moving around like usual."

"Really?" Neal left the sink and joined me. He stroked the hair from my face. "You look a little pale. Do you think you should call Dr. Starre?"

Dr. Starre had one of the most well known practices in Los Angeles. Several of my friends and members of my family were also his patients. We agreed he was handsome yet ragged from too many years of delivering babies in the middle of the night. On the rare occasion when he straightened his hunched back, his deeply tanned skin, sandy blond shoulder length hair and slate colored eyes gave him poster boy looks of a Southern California beach boy. To me, he was a hero having helped me deliver Bobby into the world -- a tedious eighteen-hour stretch.

As Neal suggested, I called and Dr. Starre told me to come right in. As I entered the waiting room, I found myself in the middle of a class session Dr. Starre was teaching for six expectant couples. A redheaded woman in a leopard print shirt was talking, "Should I discontinue coloring my hair?"

"I'll be back in just a couple minutes," Dr. Starre told them as he escorted me to an examining room.

"I'm really sorry for disturbing your class."

"Don't worry about it. Let's do a non stress test and see what's going on."

He smiled and braced my shoulder with his muscular hand, supporting me as I lay back on the examining table. I hiked up the hem of my shirt, exposing my bare belly with its brown line running from navel to pubic hair, the linea nigra, prominent enough to land a jet on. Caused by hyper pigmentation, the linea nigra, along with swollen breasts and prominent leg veins, reminded me daily of what it meant to carry a baby. To perform the non stress test, Dr. Starre used a tocodynameter that monitors a fetus's heart rate while recording uterine contractions and fetal movement. Dr. Starre gently wrapped the wide black belt, not unlike a car lap belt, around my midsection. Instead of a buckle there was a small, lightweight, black plastic box he slid this way and that before he was satisfied he was getting a clear reading. A couple of feet away another black box, about the size of a card deck, displayed the results of the reading in bright red digital numbers. Connected to the readout box was a special printer; as paper rolled out of it, a needle scribbled spiked lines up and down like a lie detector test. Beside the printer was a speaker where I could hear my baby's heart beat which I found most reassuring of all.

Non stress tests were a routine part of my pregnancy care. Studies claim only five stillborns will take place in a thousand cases if a patient passes the non stress test.

"Maybe you have food poisoning. What'd you eat today?"

"Pasta and spinach for lunch. Couldn't touch dinner."

"Bet you're going into labor soon. What were you today? Two centimeters dilated?"

"That's right."

"Some babies get real quiet at the onset of labor." His eyes flickered briefly over the paper tape spewing from the printer. "Relax. I'll check back soon."

He went back down the hallway, out of sight. I took slow, shallow breaths hoping I wouldn't vomit right there on Dr. Starre's office floor. Alone in the examining room, I noticed the pink-and-green patterned wallpaper. My Dad, a retired dentist, applied pale green wallpaper in his examining rooms. "Green is a soothing color to patients," he'd always say. Naturally, my eyes shifted to the flashing red numbers of the digital readout. I blinked, thinking I was seeing funny. The numbers were flat-lining every few seconds. Alarm slowly spread out from my stomach to my limbs like batter in a hot skillet, shapeless and uncontrollable. Again a number appeared and then - nothing. In the dozens of stress tests I'd had, there wasn't one I could recall seeing that phenomenon. I coughed back a wave of nausea, setting off a loud, static rumble on the monitor loud enough to be heard down the hall in the waiting room. Dr. Starre came rushing back.

"Are you all right?"

"What's wrong? Why does her heartbeat stop and start?"

He gave a cursory glance at the digital numbers.

"That's the baby moving out of range of the monitor."

Was that annoyance I sensed in his voice?

"But I haven't felt her move. Not once."

Dr. Starre checked the paper tape as it continued to spew from the machine. "Don't worry, Cynthia. She's moving a lot."

"This is the time of day when she goes nuts moving around and I'm not feeling anything!"

He watched the monitor. "Come on! You don't feel that?" His irritation was as easy to read as a billboard.

I shrugged, a little self-conscious. "Not really."

Dr. Starre opened a drawer and palmed an instrument known as an EAL, or electronic artificial larynx, which he placed against my belly. Not having seen one before, I tried to figure out its purpose. Suddenly, Dr. Starre flipped a switch and *zap* the device delivered an audible *buzz* like a ramped-up electric razor. I nearly jumped out of my skin. The baby flinched hard and I winced as a sharp contraction followed.

"Okay. I definitely felt that."

"Try to get some rest. I expect I'll be seeing you again soon."

CHAPTER 2:

MY HEARTBEAT

The night wore on and on and I continued to feel lousy. I sipped 7-Up and tried to keep still under my sheets. A leaf rustling three blocks away can awake Neal from slumber to total wakefulness. He's been a tosser and turner since I've known him. But on that night, my numerous trips to and from the bathroom, the whirr of the bathroom pocket door, even my retching did not disturb his sleep. It was as if someone cast a spell on him. Finally, I fell into an uneasy sleep.

A moment later, it seemed, Neal roused me from bed. "Eight-thirty, my love. Bobby's looking for you. I gave him his breakfast."

I sat up. "What a night. You're lucky you could sleep through it all."

"Sleep through what?"

"My getting in and out of bed all night."

"Oh, honey. Why didn't you wake me up?"

"Doesn't one of us need to be conscious when this baby's born?"

In the kitchen, I poured a glass of Martinelli's apple juice. I had no food in my stomach and was feeling light-headed. Outside, I heard Neal start up his old blue Porsche and back out of the driveway. As he accelerated up the block, the engine grew fainter and fainter.

The house was too quiet. I felt like even I wasn't supposed to be there.

The soft murmur of a Sesame Street video played in the den and I smiled when I heard Bobby giggle. I nibbled a piece of toast off Bobby's plate expecting the baby to move any minute. The phone rang, startling me.

"I thought for sure you'd be in labor this morning," my sister-in-law Hayley said.

"Me, too! Last night I thought I was coming down with something and I couldn't feel the baby, so I saw Dr. Starre. He said everything was okay."

"Jesus, Cindy! You're feeling her now, though, right?"

"Well, not exactly. But I haven't had any food..."

"I don't like the sound of this."

"Give it a couple minutes."

"Call Starre right away. And call me right back!"

Why did Hayley have to be such a drama queen? We hung up and I called Dr. Starre's office.

"Doctor says you ought to come in. Now."

Come on, baby. I ran my hand down my belly. *Let's get this show on the road.*

I called Neal, and though I tried to dissuade him, he insisted on coming home. He must have run every red light because when he showed up, I was just reaching over my abdomen to tie my tennis shoes.

At Dr. Starre's office, one of the nurses ushered me into the same examining room at the end of the hall where I'd been the previous night. The wallpaper didn't do much by way of calming me down. Women were in the other rooms with scheduled appointments, and here I was, cutting to the head of the line. It didn't sit well with me. The nurse was strapping the monitor to my belly and moved it this way and that, looking for the heartbeat. She cast her eyes down and fled the cramped room like a spooked horse. Neal and I exchanged worried glances.

I was here last night and everything was okay. The nurse doesn't know what the hell she's doing. Everything will be fine once Starre gets in here.

On cue, Dr. Starre swooped back in, gave a brief nod to Neal and me and took the monitor in his hand. He slowly edged it to the left, then to the right like a safecracker searching for the right combination. Nothing clicked. Fear throbbed in my ears. Dr. Starre settled the monitor in one place and turned the unit's volume up. Way up. Finally we heard it. A heartbeat.

"Oh, thank God," I said.

I blew out the breath I didn't realize I'd been holding in and my heart swelled with gratitude for Dr. Starre. Like he'd been a witness to a near-miss car crash, Neal kept shaking his head back and forth. Hey, I wasn't even pissed at the inept nurse who flubbed it earlier.

"Let's go in the other room. I want to do an ultrasound," Dr. Starre said. I straightened out my shorts and pulled my shirt back down over my belly. Neal held his hand against my lower back, guiding me down the hall. The examining room where the ultrasound machine was kept was only two doors away. I lay down on the table and lifted my tee shirt and slid my shorts low across my hips.

Dr. Starre didn't say anything. He was all business and I figured he was under pressure, having squeezed me in between his regularly scheduled patients. He squirted the warm, clear, conductor jelly on my belly and traced the ultrasonic probe along it, searching for the clearest view. Squinting, I tried unsuccessfully to find the baby amidst all the black and white clutter on the monitor screen. After a moment, Dr. Starre held the probe still. The nauseating pink and green walls inched together, practically squashing Neal, Dr. Starre and me into one being.

And there was my baby. I could make out her hands and her face, her image eerily still. Hello? Why wasn't Dr. Starre saying anything? There was no air in the stifling room. For fear of disturbing the image of the baby Dr. Starre held still on the ultrasound, I didn't move a muscle. The hum of the ultrasound machine was all I could hear. Dr. Starre lifted his hand, removing the ultrasound camera from my abdomen. His eyes were still on the monitor, where he had recorded a freeze frame of our girl.

"This baby is dead."

No, I thought. *That can't be right.*

Neal stepped closer to the monitor. "The heartbeat. We heard a…"

Dr. Starre cut him off. "That was Cynthia's."

Like an ox, I stared at Dr. Starre for my next cue. Go forward. Stop. Go right. Stop. For the first time in my life, I was at an absolute loss for what to do or say.

"Last night I should've done an ultrasound."

"I don't understand," I stammered.

"We'll know more in time. But for right now, we need to deliver this baby. Meet me at Westside."

Neal slid his arm around my waist and supported me out of the room. Dr. Starre gestured toward a back corridor.

"Use the back hallway so you won't have to pass through the waiting room and see expectant mothers."

Huh? Back hallway. Why should I care if I saw expectant mothers? Sometime later I realized it was the expectant mothers he tried to shield from me. Neal steered me down the back hallway and I remember passing a few stricken faces on the girls who worked the front office. I felt like a movie camera, panning across their reactions, recording something awful. Of course, *I* was the something awful.

As instructed, we bypassed the waiting room, but the door separating it from the hallway casually swung open and I glimpsed a pregnant woman reading a magazine before Neal had me motoring along and out the back door. My eyes squinted shut like I'd been slapped from the sun-glare. The sense of complete disorientation continued. Scattered images are all I remember. My legs curled up against me in the low front seat of the car. Neal's fingers clenched around the stick shift. Tears on his cheeks.

At the maternity ward a big-boned nurse with large, round glasses hugged me like a long-lost daughter. My arms hung limply at my sides. What the hell is happening here? Owl Eyes spoke. "Follow me. We're giving you a room in the maternity ward so you can be with all the other mothers." She stressed "other mothers" like it was a rehearsed line in a play. She was so fake, and so bizarre to look at, I toyed with the idea of pinching myself.

While we lingered in the hallway, Dr. Starre arrived. Neal and I were holding hands like lost children. "The delivery is not going to be painful. I promise." I floated along in a stupor of confusion and dread. Dr. Starre said the baby had to be delivered. My mind set a course on delivering the baby. I gave no thought to anything else. Who else could I trust? Trust him.

In about half the stillborn cases in the United States, many mothers don't even realize they've lost a child for days or even weeks. When a fetus dies, it's often without any warning, in a pregnancy that had seemed totally normal up to that point. Unfortunately, a woman's body has no automatic response, no built-in mechanism for delivering the baby.

To this day, I have no idea what caused me to become violently ill for twelve hours nor if there was a connection between my baby's distress and my illness. All I know is, over the course of nine months, I had become in tune with Samantha's cycles. The roundness of her face and the shape of her body became more familiar through each ultrasound viewing. I sang songs to her and she was my girl. If I sensed something ominous, it was quelled by Dr. Starre's assessment. Like Shakespeare's Macbeth, who was convinced by his trusted advisors, the witches, that he was safe as long as the forest never moved, I was lulled into thinking all was well and my child would never cease to move.

The nurses showed me to my private room, which was dim, somber and windowless. They gave me a cotton gown and I changed out of my maternity clothes and slipped it on. Neal took my clothes from me and stashed them in a blue hospital-issue plastic bag. The nurses poked my forearm with a needle and I didn't blink. They hooked me up to an intravenous pitocin drip to jump-start labor into full speed.

During the series of events, I completely lost track of time. Dr. Starre came in and stood at the foot of the bed. "Breaking the bag of waters ought to speed labor along." He put a hand on each calf and spread my legs. The nurse, Maria, was a friendly face who had assisted in Bobby's delivery.

"I am terribly sorry for what has happened," she said.

"Thank you."

She handed Dr. Starre a long thin tool resembling a knitting needle. Numb from shock, I didn't feel a thing when Dr. Starre inserted the tool inside me and punctured the bag of waters. A warm liquid poured out of me.

"Meconium was released," Dr. Starre said. His voice was grave. His manner reminded me of the kid who is sent to the principal's office and doesn't question it. Meconium is a black, tarry, substance made of mucus and bile - a waste product only expelled in utero when a fetus is in distress. My mind went to work: How long had she been in trouble? When did she actually die? Did she suffer? Oh, God. Did she?

My mind turned to the immediate: Labor. I didn't cry. I wasn't in hysterics. When the anesthesiologist came in, Dr. Starre instructed me to get on my side. Two and a half years earlier, I'd done all this during labor with Bobby. Back then, having a needle inserted into my spine scared the dickens out of me. This time around, it was about as intimidating as a manicure.

15

Dr. Starre's left hand steadied my head, while the other braced my back. I felt his strong fingers tremble. Instinctively, I raised my arm and held his hand. Why did I want to reach out to him? Why did his shaking hands stir me so? In some sense, this was his baby, too.

Maria helped the anesthesiologist gather his equipment and they both left the room. Neal said, "Are you okay for a couple of minutes? I want to talk to your Mom and Dad."

"Go ahead. It's alright." Neal kissed my forehead and stepped out. Alone in the darkened room with Dr. Starre, I lay still while he sat on the edge of my bed. How long had I been here? When I'd first arrived, Neal had taken my watch from me as the nurses suggested. The under-counter fluorescent lights cast a weird greenish glow in the room. Dr. Starre shifted on the bed.

"This was my fault. I should've delivered this baby last night."

He couldn't possibly mean that. Did he think I blamed him?

"You took a good look at me, right? If that was the call, you'd have made it."

He took a deep breath, almost talking to himself. "I should've done an ultrasound."

Given that Los Angeles is the sue-happiest town in the nation, I saw his confession as tantamount to a fireman entering a burning building; I admired the heroism and feared for his self-destruction. It had all the makings of an explanation but I wasn't convinced he was to blame. He had been my gynecologist for years prior to my getting pregnant with Bobby and I had always found him to be attentive and caring. How could I suddenly buy into him making a mistake as horrendous as this one?

My cervix was ripe, and where it had previously taken me eighteen hours to deliver Bobby, this labor and delivery took only three. And it didn't hurt in any conventional way. When Dr. Starre told me I could push, a tremor of fear pulsed through me. What if my baby was deformed? After all, something had gone wrong. I didn't know how wrong.

The panic flared up in my eyes as I started to push the baby out. Neal took one look at me and saw the fear. "It's okay."

I stared back at him, frozen with alarm. He fixed me with a stern look. "It's *okay.*"

Astonished, I peered down between my thighs and saw her, all curvy, white and feminine in the palms of Dr. Starre's hands. She had plump little thighs with a couple rolls of fat. Her abdomen was long and rather slim. Her hands were pudgy and the nails needed a trim. Her hair stood out, dark brown against her fair face. Her eyes were still closed. Dr. Starre startled me as he swiftly cut the umbilical cord. My mouth started to open to object - wasn't that Neal's job?

When he handed her to me I was struck by how light she felt. A sleeping baby has weight and the reassuring motion of its chest rising and falling with each delicate breath. She was lighter than a shadow, an astonishingly beautiful, empty shell. It was unbearable to hold her because it was such a cheat; it wasn't her anymore. The baby I'd loved and held inside of me was gone. The spark that was my baby's life, the rhythms of her sleep and her play, all that I'd learned to love, all the dreams I had for her and for us, had simply vanished overnight. Her face looked a lot like Bobby's; it was heart-shaped and full-cheeked. I stared at her lips. They weren't pink like a newborn's; they were a deep plum color like one of my lipsticks. In a moment's time, I handed her body back to Neal. It felt unsettling to hold this featherweight body in my arms as if it were my baby.

"She's not here," I whispered.

Dr. Starre's voice brought me back to the present. "We need to deliver the afterbirth. A couple more pushes…" My feeble attempts didn't get the job done.

"You've run out of steam," Dr. Starre said. His left hand firmly massaged my belly while his right hand coaxed out the afterbirth. Passive as a pigeon, I was stitched up, cleaned up and fussed over.

"See this little kink?" Dr. Starre showed us the umbilical cord. "I think this may be where the cord twisted and cut off her oxygen." My eyes scanned the cord but I could not detect any such kink in its smooth, shiny surface. Unsure, Neal squinted and thought maybe he could see something. "So the cord wasn't wrapped around her neck or anything?" Neal said.

"But it could have twisted like a garden hose, and cut off her circulation. We should have an autopsy performed to rule out anything else for future pregnancies." Dr. Starre looked at me for a moment then turned his attention to Maria, gave her some instructions and left.

Out of nowhere, the fatigue slammed me. I hadn't slept the night before and the physical exertion of delivering a dead child finally knocked me down. My body began to shake and my teeth were clattering. It was all I could do to say one sentence: "I'm cold." Neal approached one of the nurses and asked her for an extra blanket.

She quickly brought me one; it had been heated, I noticed. It wasn't enough, though. No matter how many warm blankets the nurses put over me, I still shook like I was standing naked in the sleet.

The hub of activity had no effect on me until one of the nurses I did not recognize wheeled a plastic bassinet into the room and parked it at the foot of my bed. I raised myself up on my elbows and saw through the clear plastic to a little lump covered with blankets. Neal and I exchanged an unsettled look.

"Excuse me?" I called softly to the nurse.

"Yes?"

"Can you please move her?"

She froze in her tracks.

"Some families want to spend time with their babies."

"Take her out of here," I said. My voice was menacing as a growl.

"Wouldn't you like a few minutes alone with --," she persisted.

"No. I wouldn't!"

My eyes tracked her like a rifle sight as she backed up and wheeled the baby out like she was maneuvering a grocery cart through a tight space.

I sighed, glad she and the bassinet were out of sight. Unfortunately, when the door to my dim room swung open it was the nurse again.

"We're taking some pictures of her. Hospital policy."

Nurses took photos of dead babies? Good God.

"It's totally your decision as to whether you want to see them or not. If you do, they'll be ready in about a week. We'll call you."

Neal looked as surprised as I was.

"Why in the world are you taking pictures of...I mean, really, isn't this a little morbid?" I said. *Sick*, not "morbid", is what I had on the tip of my tongue.

"A lot of parents want them."

If hanging on to that were your only memory, I'd rather forget.

In my fog of confusion, I'd almost forgotten my family was right outside in the hallway. They all came in - my Mom and Dad, Greg, Hayley, and Neal surrounded me in the bed like a protective fortress. Hayley took Neal aside and whispered, "If you want to see the baby again you should go now." He gave her a curious look.

Later, Neal shared that when he went across the hall, the nurses weren't just taking photos - they were applying make-up to the baby's face.

The overwhelming realization that something really bad could happen to my babies seized me. It felt like a lifetime ago that Dr. Starre had taken Neal and I into the examining room and shown us the ultrasound.

I turned to my Mom. "Bobby's alone with the housekeeper. I need to get to him." Dr. Starre wasn't about to release me from the hospital yet.

"I'll go now and take care of him," Mom said. She fished through her purse for the parking ticket and left right away. I calmed down. She'd lie before an oncoming train for her grandkids.

"Are you okay for a few minutes? I need to call my Mom and sister...and the office, too, I guess," Neal said.

"Sure. Go ahead."

"We'll be here. Go make your calls," my Dad said.

My mother and father in-law from New York had pre-purchased airline tickets in anticipation of the birth of our baby and were due out to Los Angeles in two weeks. When Neal told them what had taken place, they said they'd keep to their original plans of visiting in a couple weeks.

Neal was logical, making calls in an orderly fashion. My head was spinning. I wasn't ready, not by a long shot, to start dealing with the world and telling anyone what happened. With the patience and strength of a live oak, Neal stood steady. He kept his emotions in check long enough to deal with the ordeal of placing calls to his family on the East Coast and to a colleague at work.

His level-headedness never wavered as the hospital presented us with a flurry of papers to be signed. Neal sifted through them all and helped explain them to me while I signed them. My hand wavered over the signature line of the permission agreement for having an autopsy performed. Taking in that she was gone was one thing, having her torn apart was another.

When I was sixteen years old, the dean of the USC Dental School, a pal of my Dad's, took a shine to me and invited me to campus for lunch and a tour. The labs and classrooms were what I expected to see, but the cadaver lab was another story. The neck down was first semester, the neck up, second semester. This was Fall and the head and neck were sealed up in some kind of opaque plastic. The image of my daughter on an examining table sent a deep chill through me.

More paperwork and more calls were necessary to get the funeral underway. I was in no condition to handle it and I watched Neal carefully consider each piece of paper he read and signed. While still in the hospital, we had to choose a name for the death certificate for the state of California. "Samantha" and "Joelle" were our favorites and we had planned to finalize her name once we saw her little face. We ended up choosing "Samantha" (Sam had been the name of both my grandfathers) and in my secret heart I hoped one day there would be a Joelle, too.

My Dad popped his head in. "Rabbi Stern is here. Is it okay if he comes in?"

"I guess so."

The rabbi sat in a chair beside my bed. During Hebrew school, he led all the services and got to know all the students. His black hair was thinning and streaked silver. He didn't stand quite as tall as I remembered him but he had always been sincere and kind. Neal sat on the bed beside me. The lights were low in this windowless chamber where I felt more like a prisoner than a patient. "I'm so sorry for what has happened. No one can understand the kind of pain you're going through."

"Thank you for coming by," Neal said.

"In time, you'll heal. You're young. The two of you have your whole lives ahead of you. There's one thing I want you two to promise me."

"Yes?" I said.

"Don't blame each other for what's happened."

"Okay, Rabbi," Neal answered.

"Listen to me. When tragedy strikes a husband and wife want to blame someone. The easiest target is each other. What happened to you could not be helped. Please, Neal. Cindy. Whatever you do, don't blame each other."

The last time I'd held a personal audience with a rabbi was five years earlier with Rabbi Feldman, who had officiated at our wedding. Rabbi Feldman had written books and articles, and had a reputation as a humorous and scholarly cleric. Though he'd married my folks, and my brother and Hayley, I barely knew him. Neal and I weren't very observant Jews; we went to High Holiday services, we had a Passover Seder, and we lit candles on Hanukah. Period. If I happened to be at the bakery on a Friday, I'd pick up a challah, braided egg bread traditionally eaten on Shabbat. My folks called Rabbi Stern and, I learned later, Feldman, too. When Rabbi Stern left, he promised to visit us again soon.

I swung my legs over the side of the bed and shuffled to the bathroom. Neal moved to support me and I waved him off but the energy I summoned to get me across the room felt like I was hauling a bear carcass instead of my own body. As I peed, a mess of blood, bright and startling as a pitcher of fruit punch, filled the bowl. "Whoa!"

From the other side of the door I could hear Neal's footsteps striding across the room to get to me. "You okay?"

"Yeah, I'm fine." I gathered myself and fished around the rose-colored plastic container holding over-sized sanitary napkins, diapers and a sixteen-ounce squirt bottle. I filled the bottle with warm water and gently squeezed the sides of it causing water to stream between my legs. Blood kept pouring out with the water. I continued squeezing until my hand had formed a tight fist and the bottle was empty.

"You sure you're okay?" Neal was still on the other side of the door.

"I'm bleeding a lot more than I remember bleeding with Bobby. But it's okay." I secured a sanitary napkin to my panties and washed my hands.

Shivering, I got back in bed and pulled the covers up to my chin. A soft knock on the door made me look up. It was Dr. Starre, hovering in the doorway threshold. "I'm going back to the office to see a few patients, but I'll be back."

"When can I get out of here?"

He checked his watch and made some kind of calculation in his head. "Maybe four or five o'clock."

"If there's any way to make it earlier I'd really appreciate it."

"We'll just have to see how the day goes."

I nodded and he turned to leave. I called out to him.

"Do you have a sec? I wanted to ask you something."

Dr. Starre stepped inside and the door swiftly shut behind him.

"How long should I wait until I get pregnant again?" Shock and dumb hope kept me from realizing how wrecked I really was. Neal looked a little surprised to hear the question but Dr. Starre's shoulders straightened up, buoyed by the notion of it.

"After you resume a normal period. About six weeks."

"You're kidding."

"The autopsy report should be done by then. Not that I'm expecting there will be anything in there that would affect a future pregnancy."

The autopsy report. It was going to explain this mystery to me, grant me peace of mind, and even tell me whether getting pregnant again was prudent. Within its pages, I would have the concrete opinions of professionals as to *why* things went wrong. Its importance rose in my mind as conspicuous as the Goodyear blimp.

Meanwhile, my own spiritual descent began in earnest. A fault in the earth wrenched open and I was cascading into it careening off the jagged rock face, the sun dimming by the minute. Though many details not written in my journal have faded from memory, one thing about that time stands clear: Neal's strength. I might have been falling but all I had to do was open my eyes to see Neal as solid as a mountain. My gut told me that as bad as this day was, he'd never allow me to hit rock bottom.

As promised, Dr. Starre returned a few hours later and released me early. "I'll call you for your follow-up exam in four weeks and we'll do it on a day the office is closed. I want to make things as easy as possible for you."

"We appreciate that," Neal said.

"And if anything comes up before that, don't hesitate to call me, Cynthia."

One month was a lifetime away. What I was thinking was: How would Bobby react when I showed up at home, belly gone and no baby to show for it? Neal stuffed my few belongings into a duffle bag. I slipped on the elasticized shorts and orange and pink striped shirt I'd been wearing earlier that day. Their bright colors mocked my piss-poor condition. The way my maternity shirt hung too low in front gave me the impression I'd forgotten some important accessory like a belt or suspenders. I *was* missing something. My child.

The nursing shift had changed and a fresh, smiley young nurse pushed the door open to my room and wheeled in a wheelchair for me. "Congratulations on the baby!" she cooed.

Neal's eyes looked into mine, helpless.

Perfect, I thought, as I slumped into the wheelchair, crossing my empty arms in front of me like a shield.

CHAPTER 3:

HOME

The Westside Regional Hospital sent me clamoring for the familiarity of Bobby's hugs, my own shower and my own sheets. Westside Regional represented the creepiest of haunted houses and I vowed to never step foot there again. As soon as I walked through my side door, Bobby ran to me and hugged me around the thighs. "Momeeee!"

My fears that he would bombard me with questions about the baby I was unprepared to answer were unwarranted. He just wanted to be close, to tell me about the games he'd been playing with my Mom and the newest Sesame Street video he'd watched. Neal picked Bobby up in his arms. "Mommy needs to take a nap," Neal said. Bobby pinched Neal's nose in response. "Meeep!" Neal called out in a nasal voice and Bobby broke into a giggle fit.

In the shower, I turned the faucet as hot as I could stand in an effort to wash the hospital smell out of my hair and off my skin. Drying off, I felt a little more myself until I saw blood running in a thin ribbon down my inner thighs. I seized a sanitary napkin and cleaned myself up. Deep sobs I'd been holding back worked themselves loose. Mom was nearer than I thought, and came rushing to me. She smoothed my hair away from my face. "No, my darling. You mustn't do that. Don't cry your *kishkas* out."

But it felt right to be crying my guts out. And I hadn't had a moment alone since Dr. Starre had said, "This baby is dead."

She put her arms around me, trying to calm me down.

"I'm sorry, Mom. I can't help it."

She kissed my cheek and let me finish putting on my sleepwear. I leaned over the sink and splashed cold water over and over on my face until I felt the hot tears stop. When I got out of the bathroom, the covers of my bed had been pulled back for me like when I was a little girl. For once in my life, I didn't mind being treated like a child.

Bobby climbed onto the bed with me, nestled into my arms and I breathed in his hair, smelling of the sun, and brushed my lips against his snowy forehead, smooth and silky as a seal's pelt. Everything I needed was right there in my bed.

That night, Neal and I got into bed and I pulled the covers tight around me. Even though I was home, in my own bed, the landscape of everything I thought I knew had changed. Not only did my own room feel unfamiliar, I knew that I was never going to be the same person I'd been the day before. Because I wasn't one hundred percent sure of what that meant, a seed of fear began to germinate in my chest. Intuition told me to flee to a safer place. Where was that place? I had no idea. Neal was right next to me, his breathing rhythmic, deep and reassuring. I fell asleep.

Mine was a dreamless void and when morning light coaxed open my eyes, my windows, sans shades, revealed a monotone sky. Yesterday's events cascaded down like a rockslide, each memory a flinty stone grazing me. The song of the morning - loud, aggressive crows and singsong sparrows -came through my window but I missed the high-pitched chirps of the baby birds that had been living in a nest high in the rafters of our backhouse. Still in my boxers and tank top, I crept out my bedroom doors to look for them, knowing they were too young to have flown off by themselves. My fingers grasped the edge of the metal screen door as I eased it closed behind me. The brick patio was cold and rough against the balls of my feet as I moved closer to the nest and strained to hear the chirps. I paused below the twiggy basket woven with bits of yarn, waiting. Waiting. Waiting for something I knew wasn't there.

Back inside, I crept down the hallway toward Bobby's room - to my right was Samantha's room. Soft morning light made the lemon-yellow walls glow. For a second, I caught a glimpse of the rocking chair on the far end of the room and diapers stacked neatly on the changing table. Not knowing what else to do, I closed the door.

Late afternoon slunk up like a predator and it was darker than the hour called for. My Mom and I were seated in the den on the black leather sofa, staring out the window. A day earlier, I had been reclined on this same sofa wondering if I had the flu. My Mom's eyes were red and puffy. She obviously had been crying her insides out against the advice she'd given me not to do so. All the same, it was comforting to have her by my side even if we weren't saying much. The kitchen table had flowers, cookie platters and boxes of muffins from sympathetic friends and family. My Mom nervously snatched a mini-muffin off the tray and popped it whole into her mouth.

Bobby banged away on an electronic keyboard we'd originally bought him as a gift from "the baby". Of course, now we just gave it to him as a surprise and we didn't make any mention of the baby. In the dimming light of day I remembered the timer for the lights was broken and I toyed with the idea of calling our electrician. If all had gone according to plan, I should have been breastfeeding, changing diapers, burping the baby, rocking in the rocker, writing thank you notes.

I was vaguely aware of an ache in my breasts and dimly recalled the nurses suggesting ice packs to reduce milk production. It all felt like way too much work. Neal shuffled in from the bedroom and I noted the overall look of exhaustion in his posture. He sifted through our CD collection on the shelf and slid one into the CD player.

"Is it okay if I call the electrician to fix the timer?" I asked.

"Do we need to do the lights now?" he said in a low voice.

What exactly are we supposed to be doing now? I thought to myself. *Was there some kind of unspoken protocol?*

"Beats sitting in the dark."

As if on cue, the haunting theme music from the soundtrack *Gettysburg* began to play. Neal had worked on the film and the producers had sent him a box full of theme products.

Mom poured me some tea and a set a little dish in front of me with a chocolate muffin on it.

"Eat something. You need to get your strength back."

I held the hot mug of tea in my hands and looked at my Mom. The dark music swelled dramatically.

"What do I say to the electrician when he asks about the baby?"

She picked up another muffin. "Let me think about that."

"Do you believe this music?" I whispered.

"Where's the rope? I'm ready to hang myself."

We cracked weak smiles. Neal paced by us on his way to the kitchen.

"The Baumans sent us the muffins. I think there's a lemon poppy seed one in there you'd like. And love, could you please put something else on? We're going nuts in here listening to this."

"Yeah, sure." He smiled sheepishly. He must have realized the music was a little over the top but we were reeling from shock, feeling our way as we went along.

My brother tapped on the back kitchen door reserved for family and good friends. Neal let him in and they hugged.

"How are you?" Greg asked him.

"I don't know. I really don't."

Greg was holding a small white paper bag that I recognized from the pharmacy. In it was a bottle of Vicodin, which Dr. Starre had prescribed "for pain." The cramps of my uterus shrinking back to size were painful only in an irritating kind of way. My brother's smooth, olive-colored face was unusually blotchy. His easy smile looked painted on. By habit, he swung open the refrigerator door, glanced at the shelves without really seeing them, and just as quickly closed it.

"Mom filled it. Nothing looks good?" I asked.

"Not hungry, I guess," he said.

I held up the bag he'd brought me. "Thanks, bro."

The phone rang and Neal answered it.

"Anything else I can do, my sister?"

Bobby came running in and Greg grabbed him and picked him up. "Who's your favorite uncle?"

"Uncle Greg!"

"Who's your only uncle?"

"Uncle Greg!"

He kissed Bobby and set him down. Bobby went straight for a chocolate chip muffin and I didn't stop him though it was getting close to dinnertime. Muffin in hand, he wandered away, back to the new keyboard.

"Can you believe Bobby hasn't asked us where the baby is?" I said. "It's all we've been talking about here for months."

"He and Garrett are only two and a half. A baby's kind of an abstract thing to a kid until they actually see them," Greg paused. "Maybe it's best not to say anything at all?"

"But you're going to, right?"

"Maybe when they're older."

"They're going to hear one way or another. Eventually."

"Mom and Dad always sheltered us from bad stuff."

I cracked a smile. "And what good did it do?"

Neal came back with the portable phone in his hand. "It's Rachel."

"You better take that," Greg said. He gave me a squeeze, shook Neal's hand and left.

Rachel and I went way back in a friendship that began in eleventh grade English. We had nicknames for each other based on the book *Crime and Punishment* which we'd loved for its dark, troubled main character, Rodion Romanavich Raskolnikov. We had run through the hills of Benedict Canyon listening to The Who or Oingo Boingo on our Walkmans. We shared lip-gloss and wore the same-sized clothes.

After high school graduation we traveled to Europe together, and when we returned, around the time of my eighteenth birthday, we shopped for Trojans - just in case.

Neal gave me a quizzical look, still holding the phone out to me. *What do I say? How am I supposed to do this?*

"Hello?"

"No baby yet, Rodya! I thought I'd get your answering machine for sure," she teased.

"Listen, Fedya. I've got some really bad news." I swallowed hard. Neal was nearby but I kept my eyes cast to the floor. "She died yesterday."

"What?" Her voice was uncharacteristically high-pitched.

"I had a stillborn."

"Oh my God. Oh my *God*!"

"We're not sure what happened yet. Probably a cord accident." The tears came and I struggled to get the words out. "I can't talk about this right now."

"Can I call you later? Is it okay if I give you a call later?"

"Yeah, okay." I hung up and cried.

I remembered the pills Greg brought and I quickly filled a glass of water and downed one. *Maybe they'll numb my senses or make me sleep.* In the yard, I saw the lights were shining brightly and I did not care.

Later, I lay in bed hoping for the "Ahhhh" moment of relief from the Vicodin that never came. My uterus suddenly throbbed, a sensation similar to a baby's movements. My hand slid down over my belly, the tissue loose and foreign to my touch, like a balloon that had been blown up, stretched tight and then deflated. My brain flipped over, trying to make sense of the impossible. There can't be a baby. The twinge strengthened into a wave of cramps. I pulled the covers over my head and cried until I couldn't breathe, until I couldn't think, until, finally, I couldn't cry any more.

CHAPTER 4:

MOTHER'S DAY

Four days passed and I did not step foot away from home. Food showed up in the refrigerator, laundry was done and flowers were arranged on the table. Neal stayed home from work. So caught up in my own sadness, I don't remember what he did to pass the time.

The Sunday paper came and I realized it was Mother's Day. My Mom and Dad offered to have our family over for a quiet brunch at their house or even out at a restaurant but nothing felt right and I turned them down. At the time, my breasts had filled with milk and I was carrying around surgical gloves filled with ice against my chest in an effort to curb more milk production. Ice or no ice, my breasts were so tender I yelped in pain when one of my uncles stopped by and gave me a hug.

When my uncle left, Neal suggested we catch a movie, just the two of us. The idea of being anonymous, sitting in the dark and escaping all the typical Mother's Day activities sounded like a good idea. I tossed the ice into the sink and went to call my Mom who had offered to baby sit for us.

On our way out, I heard the phone ring. Thinking it might be my Mom with a question, I turned on my heel and ran back to answer it.

It was one of the moms from the Mommy & Me classes where I took Bobby. She had heard the news.

"I am so sorry."

"Thanks. Thanks a lot." I really did not want to hear this, or be late to the movie.

"But at least it didn't happen today. Mother's Day."

Her comment baffled me. "I never really thought about that."

"That would've made matters even worse," she said.

Angry tears pooled in the corners of my eyes. I did my best to gentle the tone of my voice. "We're actually on our way out. I really need to run."

She was one of the first people to say something strangely hurtful. A few weeks earlier, she had surprised me at Mommy & Me class with a gift, a baby journal, to record milestones in the pregnancy and "firsts" for the newborn. Her call reminded me of the journal and how I'd already written many entries about the progress of the pregnancy in it. I suddenly felt the punch of my missing baby, realizing all over again there would be no first word, first smile, first tooth.

Turned out there was time for Neal and I to mill around before the movie began. He held my hand as we wove in and out of people on the Promenade in Santa Monica. We walked past bookstores and coffee houses until we got to *The Broadway Deli*. We dodged through the crowd and found two seats at the counter where we could watch the cooks boil pasta, grill burgers and chop salads in a blur of never-ending movements.

For some strange reason, I brought my 35mm camera. Taking pictures was a passion but why did I choose to take a picture of Neal grieving in a public place? He was unshaven, his posture slumped and he wore dark glasses indoors. Did I need to convince myself that this nightmare was real? I don't think we said one word to each other but it was good just to sit side by side and pick at our lunch.

Afterwards, we walked to a nearby theater to see *Crimson Tide* and I have to admit that watching Denzel Washington on the big screen temporarily took my mind off my troubles. Each time Samantha came to mind, I pushed her away and lost myself in the story on film. To sit in a cool, dark theater surrounded by strangers, none of whom made my business their concern, was soothing. Escape seemed a perfectly acceptable solution to the unthinkable. In trying terribly hard to forget I managed to do one thing: Make the moment of Samantha's death a permanent guest in my mind.

As the film ended and the credits rolled, I kept seeing Dr. Starre's face and hearing his voice drowning out the noise of the excited movie crowd moving around me. When Neal and I emerged from the darkness of the theater, instead of squinting from sunlight, I felt the chill of remembering the freeze-frame ultrasound image of my dead child. Neal pulled me out of the building and away from the ghosts.

As we made our way to the public parking structure, there was a familiar face in the crowd smiling at me. It was out of context but I immediately recognized Bobby's pediatrician, an incredibly personable and capable man. He was surprised to see us; he had been expecting a happy call from us, summoning him to the hospital to check out the new baby. A few feet away, his wife and two children were waiting for him in front of a toy store.

"What should I say to Bobby?" I asked him.

"Or is it best to say nothing and try to act as if nothing happened?" Neal said.

Stung, I shot Neal a look. Samantha was a part of our lives and I wasn't about to dismiss her memory.

"Do whatever feels right," he said. "If he wants to sleep in your bed, if he wants to stay home instead of going out…whatever it is, give him and you as much slack as needed."

"Will this have a big impact on him?" Neal asked.

"Why don't you call my office for Jackie Redmon's number? She's a great therapist we refer out to all the time."

"Thanks so much. I'll call Monday," I said.

"Do you mind my asking? Who was your obstetrician?"

"Dr. Starre."

"I've heard of him. He's supposed to be very good."

"Oh, he is."

This was the first time I had defended Dr. Starre. From the corner of my eye, I thought Neal gave me a funny look but we didn't discuss it.

When we got home there were flowers by the front door that had been delivered in our absence. The card read: "Hope you are feeling better. Love, Dr. Starre."

"That was awfully nice of him to send these."

"Uh, huh." Neal didn't give them a second look.

"Well, he didn't have to send anything, right?"

Chapter 5:

The Shadow

Brrring! The phone. I was at my desk and had to decide whether or not to answer it. *Brrring!* Fifty-fifty it was someone who didn't know what happened yet. *Brrring!* "Hello?"

"Good morning, honey. I was thinking…do you want me to buy a little dress…for Samantha?"

"Um, what for, Mom?"

She stumbled over her words, "For the, for when, you know, the funeral."

"Oh." I paused. "No. I don't think so. It's not like anyone's going to see it. Not even her."

"Okay."

"Okay."

Was I making the right decision? I hadn't been giving any thought to the funeral though it was only a day away. Did I really want my Mom driving to a department store with the goal of buying cute infant clothes for a baby she would never hold or see? The coffin was going to be sealed, right? After all, the baby had been through an autopsy. These thoughts started to overwhelm me and I felt hollowed out like a tree infested with termites, like I could topple over any minute. My Mom's voice, gentle and soft, came through again over the telephone.

"You're sure?"

"Do you think I should?"

"It's really your decision. I don't think it matters too much one way or another."

"Don't bother, then," I said.

We confirmed what time we'd be leaving for the burial before we hung up. I sat at my desk thinking about what was folded in the bottom left hand drawer of my mahogany dresser, the one that once belonged to my Dad's parents. Tucked beneath my running shorts were two tiny dresses I'd bought at a designer clothing sale. One was an eggshell-colored dress in a cowgirl pattern. The other was a pale pink, frilly number, impractical and irresistible. They were too big for an infant; maybe they'd fit a six-month-old. When I bought them I lied to myself saying I'd give them away as presents when I'd really wanted them for Samantha.

Jewish tradition dictates one doesn't buy anything for an unborn child. Of course, these days, lots of Jewish moms-to-be register for gifts and have baby showers. The irony that I actually would be wrapping up the two little dresses for someone else's daughter was devastating. I pushed aside the image of Samantha wrapped in the standard-issue paper jacket and blanket from the hospital.

A day later, while getting ready for the funeral, I was still pushing unpleasant thoughts from my mind. How I accomplished this was by running late. Really, really late. Neal is Mr. Punctuality and my stalling was beginning to tick him off. Searching through my maternity dresses for an appropriate outfit was a convenient excuse not to dress at all. Neal was pacing back and forth from the kitchen to our bedroom, checking my sorry progress. My grandmother Nanny's coral earrings dangled from my ears and I hoped that somehow her spirit would give me the strength to get through this day.

Nanny had been through a lot; she was a young girl when her parents died. Her older sister who she adored took her in. She spent her teenage years helping to raise her numerous nieces and nephews including one who was stricken by tuberculosis. Her education had been cut short but she found other outlets to experience the world. She sought work as an extra in the silent movies like *Birth of a Nation*. She learned to cook mouth-watering kreplach soup and fluffy matzo balls. When she married my grandfather and had her own children, her goal was that they be educated. While my mind actively sifted through the past, my getting ready coasted safely to a complete stop.

"I give up," Neal said as I dawdled around in my panties, bra and coral earrings.

"O-kay!" I snapped. I finally slipped on a long-sleeved black and white dress that hung too low in the front, where my round belly used to protrude.

My brother drove us to the cemetery in Hayley's six-seat Montero. It was a private ceremony and I didn't even have my son or nephews there. None of us were prepared for Samantha's death and we were a long ways off from explaining it to the kids. Besides, I couldn't fathom alarming Bobby by seeing us all falling apart before his eyes.

The weather was movie set cliché - windy and gray. My new habit, a deep sigh, escaped me. My insides felt as cold and bottomless as a crack in a glacier. Goose bumps popped up on my legs and showed through my black tights. In the backseat, I scrunched closer to Neal for warmth. He put his arm around me and held me firmly against him. The 405 Freeway, usually choked with debris like a river after a storm, was sweeping me away like Class IV rapids. My senses, not very reliable at the time, registered danger and it occurred to me my whole family could be wiped out in a single car wreck.

These forebodings plagued me for months. They weren't panic attacks exactly, but they caused my stomach to lurch like I was inexplicably teetering atop a roller coaster at the most unexpected times.

The representative at Hillside Cemetery gave us details on how the ritual would take place and on headstone options. He explained that when a child dies, the cemetery covered the cost of the burial. I tried to express gratefulness but it rang hollow as a drum. The man wiped tears from his eyes and I looked at him a little confused.

"My daughter just lost a baby...I am so sorry that happened to you, too. It's just horrible." He pulled a hankie from his pocket and blew his nose.

Neal cleared his throat, "We're sorry to hear that you and your family are suffering, too."

Soon after we arrived, old Rabbi Feldman, the man who had married us, drove up. My parents were touched; we'd all been expecting a different rabbi since Feldman had been sickly. One rabbi or another didn't make any difference to me; I was not counting on him for solace or inspiration. My hope was that this day would be over as quickly as possible. The shock, buffering me when I went through labor and delivery, had worn off days earlier. There was nothing standing between me and the torture of placing my child's body in the ground.

As instructed, we drove our car along a paved curvy road to an area where babies and children were buried. The grounds were grass covered with trees and benches tastefully placed along the rolling hills. Different areas of the cemetery had names like "Eternal Life" and "Oakwood." We were directed to "Sunland", a flat lot about thirty square yards.

Sunland was reserved for children and babies who had died. As soon as I laid eyes on it, I felt a shadow fall across me. Maybe because Mother's Day was so recent, there were lots of toys placed beside the headstones. Another obvious thing I hadn't realized before that day was this: Families often visited their deceased relatives and friends on holidays. A gust of wind made me shudder and sent the pinwheels on the headstones spinning.

My family and I sat in folding chairs, lined up alongside the coffin and a fresh rectangular-shaped hole in the ground. Standing before us, Rabbi Feldman took a deep breath and spoke loud enough to be heard above the wind.

"In Jewish tradition, babies that don't live at least thirty days are not given a funeral. The Torah says these babies should not be grieved for. The family is not to sit *shiva*. Of course, the heart may tell us otherwise."

Sitting *shiva* is when family and friends spend seven days and nights in mourning at home. A Rabbi comes to say prayers, mirrors are covered, and family and friends keep company with the bereaved family. Almost everyone shows up with food; typical items are chocolate chip rugala, cold cuts, different kinds of fresh breads and cakes.

Rabbi Feldman recited prayers in Hebrew, which I couldn't translate. Then he uttered the mourner's prayer "...though I walk through the shadow of death..." Those words were something I always heard recited for elderly people who had passed on, never a child.

Times have changed in recent years. Traditional rituals and new rituals have been combined to deal with the loss of a newborn or stillborn. There is little distinction in medical literature between stillbirth and the death of a newborn; both are treated as the death of a baby. Certainly, a mother's physical and emotional condition and a father's connection to his baby are the same in either case. Current Jewish rituals call for a father's loss to be treated equally to a mother's loss.

Another gust of wind hit us head-on and my hair whipped my face and my dress threatened to fly up. I was shaking and crying, more miserable than I thought was possible. Neal shrugged out of his coat and placed it over my hunched shoulders. My Mom's whimpering and my Dad's sobs were enough to level me without seeing my brother shaking with grief and my tiny sister-in-law looking hopelessly lost. Fresh off his own loss, the representative was bawling, too. After the rabbi finally finished speaking, my Dad blew his nose (a five minute ordeal that would've normally had us in stitches) and cleared his throat. In a measured tone that momentarily stilled our crying he said, "As long as we remember Samantha with our love, she'll be immortal."

The Hillside representative handed me a rose, and it took me a moment to understand it was meant for me to place on the small white coffin. My hands were shaking hard and I tried to steady myself so the flower wouldn't roll off the coffin. From the wings, two guys in gardener uniforms double-checked the ropes looped beneath either side of the casket. When they were satisfied, they began slowly and evenly lowering the casket into the neat rectangular hole in the ground.

A few feet away, a shovel rested in the dirt like a dare. Without a trace of hesitation, Neal strode toward it, holding my hand. He grasped the shovel and tossed dirt down onto the coffin where it scattered with a hollow sound. He held it out to me, and together, we tossed in more dirt. Neal didn't let go of the shovel so I didn't either. We shoveled in more dirt. An overwhelming wooziness washed over me and I felt I might cascade into the hole right along with Samantha. Neal must have sensed it and he said, "Okay." He stood straight, held me around the waist with one hand and we walked over to my Mom and Dad. Neal offered them the shovel. They walked gingerly up to the hole in the ground. My Mom kept shaking her head. "We've lost a link. We've lost a link in our family chain."

The Jewish ritual of burying the dead requires that the family of the deceased, not strangers, shovel the dirt on the coffin. The idea is the dead deserve to have their loved ones perform this last task. Also, the act of tossing dirt over a coffin forces you to face the finality of a death. As definitive as hearing the hollow sound of dirt land on a wood box may be, Samantha's death was so out of the natural order of life, rituals didn't offer much solace. Where was God? What had I done to deserve this? How could I turn to the traditions of my faith when nothing made any sense?

The rest of the day was a blur. Bobby was happy, as always, to see us. I listened to him play his electronic keyboard and went along with whatever game he was up for playing. As soon as he went down for a nap, I joined him.

A few hours later, we all met up at my folks' place for dinner. Mom surprised us with a gourmet meal served in the dining room instead of the breakfast room where we usually had our family dinners. The table was set with an elegant, white lace tablecloth, Waterford crystal goblets, flowers, and fine china as if we were celebrating something. My Mom had made a lot of my favorite dishes like orange chicken and steamed asparagus. Hayley had cooked a special recipe of stuffed chicken breasts. It looked like it belonged on the pages of *Gourmet* magazine.

My core felt as if a drill had burrowed its way in, starting from my head and proceeding down into my gut and I could barely fathom putting anything in my mouth. As each platter was passed my way, I scooped a small taste onto my dish and dutifully tried a bite of everything. My mouth became the focus of my dinner, as I had to fully concentrate on the mechanics of cutting my food, chewing each piece, swallowing, and then repeating the whole process. Finally, I had to excuse myself. I walked down the hallway to my parents' bedroom, slipped my shoes off, and curled up on their bed. Someone called, "Cindy?" but I was too far-gone to pay any mind to the voice. My eyelids crashed shut like steel shades.

Later that evening when we were back at home, I shed my clothes, splashed water on my face and did a quick tooth brushing, so eager was I to get back to bed. I wore a tight tank top to sleep to support my chest, still heavy with milk. No matter that I had been asleep for an hour at my folks' house, without the benefit of sleeping pills or any other medications, my weariness took its toll and I was about to fall right back to sleep in a matter of seconds. Did I even kiss my husband goodnight? No. He wasn't even on my radar. If not for hearing something unusual, I would've been out for the count.

His normal careful working open of buttons on his starched shirts and the gentle swoosh of his hanging up his suit was replaced with the hangar clanging against its metal rod, the thump of his shirt being thrown on the floor. I raised myself on one elbow, squinting at the closet light.

"I'm cursed!" he said to himself.

"What is it, honey?"

"First I lose my Father. Now my daughter." He wiped his eyes.

My heart dropped a few notches lower. So bound up in my own sorrow, I failed to take notice of the weight my own husband had been shouldering. I patted the empty side of the bed.

"Come here, sweetheart."

Chapter 6:

Two Letters

M*ay 17, 1995*
Dear Sweet Samantha,
    *How your Father and I miss you and love you! Our days
are so emotional and spent mostly thinking of you, being frustrated and
angry at your physical absence of course, succumbing to despair because we
cannot go back into the past.*

    *Understand that we had big plans for you, my dearest. Not only did
we see you as our baby, but we also dreamed of all your future joys and
accomplishments as an adult as well. When I saw your angelic face I knew
you could have achieved anything you wanted.*

    *Don't get me wrong, I wanted to show you off in your baby-ness, too.
I fully planned to spoil you with adorable outfits and to take you on your
first trail ride. Dad would have you throwing a baseball before you'd
taken your first steps.*

    *You must know our feelings for you and that we'll think of you each
day for the rest of our lives, sweetheart.*
    Love, Mom

And so began a series of letters to Samantha that ultimately
helped me find a place to put all the love and emotion I was carrying
around. Do they read like Hemingway or Shakespeare? Not quite.

Are they something I re-read all the time? No. However, research proves writing is healing if you can bring yourself to do it. These letters were baby steps toward clearing up my confusion, helping me think straight and eventually, feeling happy.

The first journal I ever saw belonged to my grandmother Bunny, my Dad's mother. I was around seven years old and my family was downstairs waiting for Bunny to get dressed for a Sunday night dinner at a fancy restaurant. As was my habit, I went upstairs to help my grandmother check her lipstick and tell her if she had any smeared on her teeth. She reached into a desk drawer and removed a small leather-bound journal. She sat at the desk and I stood beside her, unable to read her elegant, looping handwriting. When she turned the page I saw she had a sense of humor and had pencil-sketched my grandfather -- completely naked. I giggled and so did she. Sadly, these journals were lost or destroyed upon her death.

No one suggested I start a journal but lots of people had other advice. The Rabbi hinted I ought to think about having another baby. My girlfriends gave me phone numbers of their therapists. A few bold people insisted I ought to be consulting lawyers.

How could I know what I really thought unless I committed it to paper? My emotions ruled my world and without the structure of a pen and paper to hold me straight, I would've been reduced to a crumpled heap.

The same day I wrote my first letter to Samantha, I also wrote one to Dr. Starre.

May 17, 1995

Dear Dr. Starre,

After a mostly sleepless first night home from the hospital, interrupted only by fleeting, disturbing nightmares, I awoke and peered outside my bedroom window. To my dismay, I saw that the birds that had been building a nearby nest had for some reason abandoned it.

It's been one week since then and since we've seen each other. So much has happened in our lives so quickly that it feels as though much more time has passed than the calendar indicates. The strange quality of time, however, is that each hour seems like an eternity to me.

Many times I've thought of calling you or writing you but I can't seem to focus on much except the empty feeling of not having my daughter Samantha inside me or in my arms. It's important to me, though, that I be able to express to you some of the flurry of thoughts and feelings that are coursing through me.

First off, I sense how much you are hurting, too. Certain images of you have cemented themselves in my mind…the way your hand began trembling as you tried unsuccessfully to find Samantha's heartbeat, the sound of your voice gone uncharacteristically grave as you told us our baby was dead and the look of sorrow on your face as you held her in your hands. I know how much you care for us and for our daughter and that it is not only my family and I who have been changed forever; I doubt you will ever be the same, either.

Please realize we appreciate the attention and time you spent with us during this pregnancy, as well as our previous pregnancy. For months, the highlight of our weeks was seeing you and getting progress reports on our little girl. Fact is, these good memories of Samantha make up much of what we know of her. More than our family and friends, our visits with you were times that made our daughter become more and more real to us; she was not just an abstract idea waiting to become a person – she was a member of our family.

I don't know how to explain what happened to us. I do think Samantha was in trouble the night I came to see you and the fact that I was so violently ill all evening and into the next morning makes me believe my body knew she was struggling even if my brain had no idea. If I've learned anything so far from this awful experience, it's to trust my instincts, to live by those feelings and to realize that in spite of those instincts, I have very little control in this life.

When you called the other day, you said you felt guilty and that we should blame you if we felt the need to blame anyone. I can't think of a single reason why blaming you would do any good at all. Nothing can bring my girl back to me and no one can resurrect my dreams and visions of her.

My despair is greater and heavier than any weight I've ever had to bear yet I don't take for granted my husband or my son or my family. I know they need me as much as I need them, so I can't just "check out" mentally or get in my car and drive off into the sunset.

There's comfort in the certainty that my baby knew we loved her. Never before has life presented me with the wrenching loss of a loved one. Maybe I've learned another thing from this nightmare: Love knows no boundaries.

I'm not certain when I should see you again for a check up but I believe stepping into your office may be too much for me to handle. I do want to see you again, though, so we can embrace and that you may know in your heart that I'll always treasure your being our friend and not just our doctor.

Fondest regards,

Cynthia

Neal read the letter a couple of times. I watched him bite a fingernail, in thought.

"You sure you want him to have this? I mean, it's a beautiful letter and everything, but…"

"What?"

His voice softened. "Maybe this *is* his fault, Cyn. And if we want to contact a lawyer at some point, I don't know."

"A lawyer can't bring her back."

"All the same, I want to leave my options open."

"So, do you want me to rewrite it?"

A wistful smile crossed his face and he shook his head. "Actually, it's fine as is. Nothing in there would really make any difference to a lawyer. You don't need to change anything."

The next morning, I was eager to get the letter into Dr. Starre's hands, too impatient to even wait for regular mail service. Neal offered to drive me to Dr. Starre's office. He pulled up in front of the tinted glass, two-story building. "If I'm not here when you get out, don't panic. It just means I had to go around the block."

Ba-boom, ba-boom. My heart went into overdrive with each step closer to his office. *Ba-boom, ba-boom.* And what if he saw me and wanted to talk? Face to face? Praying I didn't see anyone I knew in the waiting room, I pushed open the same door I'd walked through the night I stopped feeling Samantha move. I strode straight up to the woman at the front desk. Her hand came up to slide open the glass separating us.

"Can I help you?"

I handed her the envelope like it was a bank robber's demand note. "Could you please give this to Dr. Starre?"

"Of course. He's with patients right now, but as soon as he's out I'll give it to him."

"Thanks," I whispered as I rushed back out the door and ran to the street. Neal was there, double-parked, checking his rearview mirror for police. To me, it felt like a get-away car from a heist.

"Step on it."

In the trunk, we had several packages of diapers, as well as unopened baby bottles and rubber nipples for the relief bottles of milk Neal would have given the baby to bond with her and to give me a break from breastfeeding. They didn't belong in our house anymore and I was in a big hurry to get rid of them. We drove to a Rite Aid Drug Store off Fairfax, a place we were unlikely to see anyone we knew. When Neal parked the car, it took every ounce of strength I had to get out and close the car door behind me. In the store, we waited for a manager to process the returns. Unfortunately, they didn't carry one of the brands we brought back. "Can't you scan the code or something for a price? Please?" If he handed back those diapers I thought I'd collapse to the floor from the weight of them.

The manager thoughtfully turned the package of Huggies over in his hands.

"I think we can help you out."

CHAPTER 7:

THE RIGHT WORDS

B ruised and raw, I closed the door to my room, fell face-first onto my bed and cried. When I unfurled a short time later, I realized I was still in the exact same place as I was in before I'd let tears overwhelm me. Tears didn't make me feel much better. Feeling sorry for myself didn't feel too keen either. Worst of all, I felt out of control. Perhaps that wouldn't have bothered me quite so much if I were alone, but when Bobby caught me wiping my eyes or scurrying to another room to blow my nose and compose myself, he looked a bit frightened. His eyes would be looking for an explanation but I was at a loss for words. At that point, Neal and I made an appointment with the child therapist our pediatrician, Dr. West, had recommended.

While Bobby stayed home with a sitter, we drove along Wilshire Boulevard, a street that stretched from downtown in the East to the Pacific on the West. Somewhere along its midpoint in Westwood, I began to feel like I was peering out the window of a tour bus at men and women striding to meetings in their business suits and messengers zipping through traffic on their bikes. They looked like images from a MTV video; quick cuts of motion and color.

"Doesn't everything look like it's moving in fast motion?" I looked over at Neal in the driver's seat.

"Yeah, it does."

"I'm out of sync." I said, looking out the car window.

Jackie Redmon's office had board games and trucks and blocks stacked neatly up against one entire wall. We sat on a low, slouchy couch. Dr. Redmon surreptitiously moved a box of tissues over to our side of the coffee table.

Neal explained that two weeks earlier we'd lost our baby and we needed to find the right thing to say to our older son Bobby. After nine months of preparing him for a little sister, we just felt we had to say *something* even though he wasn't really asking us about her absence. Also, we were looking ahead and neither of us wanted a big secret to keep in our family.

"Bobby is thinking about the baby even if he doesn't have the tools yet to ask you what happened," she said.

"Wouldn't it make more sense to tell him when he's older?" Neal asked. "When he can grasp more?"

"There are ways to tell him what happened now without going into too much detail."

Greg's words echoed in my mind: "Mom and Dad always sheltered us from the bad stuff."

"I don't want to scar him for life by saying the wrong thing," I said.

Dr. Redmon suggested giving him tidbits of information, building on the foundation over time until he was mature enough to handle the entire story.

Taking her advice, Neal and I wrote down a script of what to say to Bobby. We read it out loud to one another, over and over, until we could speak the words calmly.

Remember Mommy had a big belly and the little baby was inside? Well, the baby came out of Mommy but she can't come home. Ever. The baby wasn't strong like Bobby. We still love her. Mommy and Daddy and Bobby are okay. Mommy and Daddy need to put away the little baby's things from her room.

When Neal and I got home, we squatted on the floor of Bobby's room and tried to get his attention. He was so busy playing with his trains, building bridges and moving windmills, that he didn't actually seem to be paying attention at all until I got to the sentence, "...the baby wasn't strong."

"I'm strong!" he piped up.

"You sure are," Neal said.

Then he began to demonstrate his strength by climbing up Neal's back and trying to sit on his Daddy's head.

I tried to finish my "talk" but it seemed he couldn't have cared less.

"Bobby go on Daddy's head!" he giggled.

As Neal hoisted Bobby over his head I cracked a smile. My mood lifted as I heard Bobby giggle. "Child of light. Child of love," I cooed as I mussed up Bobby's hair. When the right moment presented itself, I'd be ready for it. Until then, I was pulling up the drawbridge, maintaining the secrecy of our lost child.

It took a full seven years and someone else's tragedy to ease the drawbridge back down. A boy in our community had recently died from a concussion sustained from a baseball smacking his skull. On a late afternoon after Little League practice at La Cienega Park, Bobby and I were talking about it. Our feet crunched against the dirt path that ran alongside the baseball field.

"There's something you should know," I said. "When you were two and a half, I had a baby that died. A little girl."

"Are you serious?"

"I didn't want you to hear from someone else."

"You mean I had a sister?" He turned sideways as he walked so he could get a better look at me.

"Yes. She would've been seven."

"How'd she die?"

"It was an accident. In the womb." He gave me a confused look. "While she was still inside me."

Runners passed us going in both directions. A mom walked by, pushing a jogger-stroller in front of her. We got to the parked car and I threw his glove into the backseat.

"Could whatever happened to her happen to me?"

"No. Not a chance. See, her circulation got cut off just before she was born."

"Ugh. That's so sad."

"It's like the pumpkins we planted, right? Some of them grew and some of them never made it."

Recognition glowed in his eyes as he pictured our backyard vines. "Oh, yeah!"

I held off turning on the ignition while he buckled up his seatbelt.

"Mom?" He looked at me from under the bill of his Detroit baseball cap. "Are you still sad?"

"Nah," I lied, "it happened a long time ago."

Before this opportunity arose all those years later, I felt frustrated that the little slip of paper didn't explain the missing baby very well to Bobby and I told Dr. Redmon the plan did not work out. She suggested we have more sessions. For the next month, we met weekly and discussed the nightmares I was having, the walks I was taking, and the occasional comments from friends that were unintentionally hurting me. She kept telling me how great I was doing and I never quite believed her.

Grieving is a personal process and no one can say what will work best for another person. It's vital to be open to all opportunities to heal. Therapists can, and often do, literally save lives in their line of work. While I found Dr. Redmon's encouragement helpful and her ear valuable, I still thought something was missing. Given the choice, I chose my journal over the therapist - especially when something troubling occurred.

May 24, 1995

Samantha, dearest,

Is it possible only two weeks have passed since I saw your face for the first and last time? It just can't be. These fourteen days feel like a life spent. To have lost what should have been found has turned time into my enemy. I can't stop the feeling that you should be with me – late at night together while you nurse, in the car running around town, in your stroller on the streets in our neighborhood, playing at your Aunt and Uncle's house, being

*held non-stop by your Grandma and Grandpa, posing for my camera,
being kissed by your Dad…the list is as infinite as my love for you.*

Love, Mom

As scheduled, my in-laws arrived from New York and their mood
was upbeat. Who could blame them? New York weather was hard
on them and sunny California represented warmth and fun. Plus, any
occasion for them to see their grandchild was a kind of celebration.

The shock of the delivery, the finality of the funeral and our
weeks spent at home in a complete fog had been insulated from them
by the sheer cross-country distance. Neal and I must have appeared
to them much as before - healthy and active. Seeing Bobby made
them incredibly happy. They stayed at my folks' house and rented
a car so they could spend time at our place, coming and going as
needed. Mostly they sat on the sofa watching CNN or sitting out
back in the sunshine, reading the *Los Angeles Times*. They often ran
errands for me and played with Bobby. My Mom-in-law, Doris, also
liked answering the telephone in case it was a call from someone
back home in New York. While I was getting out of the shower one
morning, Dr. Starre called. I heard my Mom-in-law calling for me.
"Cynthia! Cynthia! It's the doctor."

Several days had passed since I dropped off his letter and I had
been expecting his call. With a towel around me, I hustled over to
the doorway to my room. "Thanks." I took the phone from her.

He wanted to know how I was feeling. "Okay," I said.

Doris stood a couple of feet away, watching my face for any
important details.

"I just wanted to tell you that I got your letter. It speaks to what a beautiful person you are."

"Oh, thanks."

"I'll keep it forever."

The water dripped off the ends of my hair onto my shoulders and down my chest.

"I meant every word," my voice sounded too soft, like it wasn't me doing the talking.

"If there's anything you need before the one month check-up..."

"Sure. I'll let you know."

The letter was meant to open up things between Dr. Starre and myself, yet we were more formal than ever with each other. When we saw one another face to face, I was certain the climate would warm up.

"Did the doctor have anything to say? Everything all right?" Doris came back to my room.

"Yes. Everything is fine." I forced a little smile to drive in the point.

Over the weekend, we made plans to have brunch with my folks and my in-laws at Brentwood Country Club. All of us faced each other around a large round table with a fresh flower arrangement in the center of it and sunlight streaming through the plate glass windows onto us. My Mom and Doris fussed over Bobby, ordering him soda and waffles with strawberries and whipped cream.

"I know this is a horrible thing that's happened but I'm still glad to be here in California, having a good time with you folks," my Mom-in-law said.

My expression went blank. I wasn't sure I'd be capable of ever having a good time again. Suddenly I heard an infant's cry. My ears pricked up. There was a tinge in my breasts that signaled potential milk let-down. My eyes scanned the nearby tables until I discovered the crying baby being rocked by his mother.

"It's good to have you here," I heard my own Mom saying to my Mother-in-law.

"Can we donate money to some organization on your behalf? We'd really like to do something."

Neal shook his head. "That's okay, Mom. Don't worry about it."

Their voices went silent as if a gunshot had been fired. Instead of a bullet, however, it was the baby's hollering that had stopped everything in its tracks. I watched the baby until he settled down and proceeded to chew his chubby, little knuckles.

My insides began to disintegrate until my bones were powder and the sensation I was sliding down, down under the table overtook me. Of course, my outward appearance hadn't changed. I was still sitting at a family brunch, looking distracted, perhaps, but I suspect that's all anyone noticed.

"Cynthia?" It was my Mom-in-law.

I pulled my gaze away from the baby. The sounds faded up again. No one else had even noticed the baby at all.

"Eat something."

"Hmm?" I turned to face her and felt tears welling up but I cleared my throat and willed them away. Ice bags on my breasts were stopping the milk let-down and daily walks were melting the extra weight away. At Sunday brunch that day, I made up my mind to cease crying.

I strangled back the tears that day. And the next. And the next. Until finally, my throat ached as if someone had punched a hole through it. I wanted to laugh when the doctor diagnosed it as a sprained throat.

My in-laws returned to New York and I could savor the time I had alone with Bobby. I'd been surrounded by family and had friends frequently calling but it was my two-and-a-half year-old boy that saved me from feeling too sorry for myself. My little pixie was a demanding boy who needed his sippy cup of juice…now! My soft kitten boy couldn't go to sleep unless I stayed in his bed half the night. My budding artist/musician/gymnast needed me to drive him to and from classes and to watch him during all his activities. He sensed my sadness, of course, and would nestle in bed with me for naps and the two of us fit together perfectly like pieces of a puzzle. His smooth creamy body was the only good thing I felt about getting close to anyone.

God knows I did not want to be intimate with my husband. How could I want him touching me? Looking into his face was seeing my own sorrow. There didn't seem to be any future I could imagine where we were together, carefree, taking physical pleasure in each other. We held each other the best we could muster - for support and for sympathy, not romance or passion. While he could tenderly kiss my mouth, his tongue was like a party crasher, uninvited and breaking some kind of unwritten code. He backed away and was incredibly patient.

When he returned from work in the evenings, he read goodnight stories to Bobby and I'd often withdraw to my bed, reading a few pages and scribbling a letter to Samantha in my journal.

I remembered Gandhi had said, "Every night I die, and every morning I'm reborn." Always striving to bridge the gap between Samantha and I, I hoped if I thought about her hard enough before I went to sleep, she would come to me in a dream - as if in my sleep I could somehow transcend the ultimate barrier between life and death.

CHAPTER 8:

A PICTURE TO HOLD

I f Samantha was in my dreams, I never remembered seeing her when I woke up. Undeterred, I hired a psychic to help me contact her. There were so many questions I wanted to ask my girl: Who are you hanging out with? Are you looking after my family and me? Why couldn't you be with me? Will you come back somehow? The psychic I called was reported to have helped the Santa Rosa Police Department solve crimes and I thought she might be useful.

Ten years earlier, when I was working at my first job as a researcher on a reality show, I had spoken to her. Doing a favor for a colleague, I promised to handle his phone while he took a break. When I answered her call, she "got a feeling". Grandma Nanny (who'd been dead for years) wanted to wish me a Happy Birthday. About my boyfriend, he was not the one.

"What do you expect to get out of this?" Neal asked.

"Answers."

"What if she says something you don't want to hear?"

"I'm willing to take the chance. Aren't you a teeny weeny bit curious?"

That same day I made my appointment and made a non-refundable credit card deposit. Soon, a small stack of papers from the psychic arrived in the mail that required my signature. One of them said, "I understand this session is for entertainment purposes only".

Turns out I wasn't as sure as about our meeting as I'd thought. I cancelled the appointment and had to forfeit the deposit. The psychic's secretary was shocked. "Do you know how difficult it is to get a time with her? She can help you! You'll really enjoy it!" Deep down, I knew I was the one in charge of making a connection with Samantha and discovering the answers to my own questions.

Foolish and optimistic, I really thought I'd find satisfaction if I focused on what went wrong, educated myself, and then life would surely go on as it had before. After all, there were many books to read on the subject of stillborns and as yet, I hadn't received the all-important autopsy.

My mind flip-flopped all the time. I had signed up for time with the psychic, then turned around and cancelled. At the hospital, I'd sworn off seeing photos of Samantha. Now I was driven to see them. Not that I'd have admitted it to anyone, but since I'd only seen her for a moment, I'd already forgotten what she looked like.

The tinted windows of Westside Regional stared down at me like a thousand shiny, black eyes and the double door entrance was more like the jaw of a giant insect. A shudder went through me as I crossed the lobby, called an elevator and stepped in. Every creak, every hum of the machinery made me jumpy. I steeled myself as I walked through the door to the office. At the desk, a woman looked up.

"My name's Cynthia Baseman. Someone left a message for me about photos?"

"Oh, yes. One moment." She put on a pair of glasses and fished through a cardboard box filled with fat, crinkly manila envelopes until she found mine. She held the package out to me and I hesitated taking it from her.

"How are they?"

She looked confused.

"Are they…" I struggled for the right word. "…good?"

She stalled, turning the envelope over in her hand. "I saw them this morning. They shot more than usual."

Uncomfortable, she shifted in her desk chair and I studied her face for any signs of what I was in for.

"There are about ten or so."

"Ten photographs."

"Eight or ten. More than usual."

Another few seconds ticked by. Finally, I snatched the envelope dangling from her fingertips, thanked her and turned on my heel to go.

"They're not bad. Really, they're not," she called after me.

Without looking back, I raised my hand to signal I'd heard her and kept on going.

Trendy design shops along Beverly Boulevard flashed by as I steered my Jeep west, the envelope riding shotgun. The Spin Doctors "Two Princes" blared loud enough on my CD player to earn me a dirty look from the woman driving her Mercedes-Benz in the next lane.

What about the box full of unclaimed envelopes? How many of us were out there? And why didn't they pick theirs up?

Roaming the house like a coyote, I straightened things that didn't need straightening and drifted from one room to the next. Finally, Neal came home at lunch to look the photos over with me. Studying the first photo was like taking a shotgun blast, point blank, to the chest.

Neal kept flipping through the stack. "My God, why did they pose her with toys?" he asked.

"I can't do this." I looked away.

We slipped the photos back into the envelope and placed it in a tall dresser drawer far from Bobby's curious reach. I knew Neal had to return to the office but I felt so lost I almost asked him to stay.

When Neal returned to work I heard the envelope talking in my dresser drawer. I sucked in a lungful of air, pulled open the drawer and slid the photos out from the envelope again. In private, I scanned over every single detail of those photos. It was my only physical reminder of what she looked like, so I placed the "best" one in a silver frame I had been given as an early baby present. In it, Samantha's arm is loosely crossed in front of her. Her wide-set eyes are closed. Her cheeks are full and flushed. Visible only from the chest up, she's wrapped in a standard-issue pink and blue striped cotton blanket.

Her face looks tranquil, like she's napping. Like she will wake up any minute.

CHAPTER 9:

TOPANGA

Neal seemed quieter than usual and I should have been paying more attention to him but the physical toll of mourning had me burned out by nightfall. I was yearning to get to sleep as soon as Bobby was in bed. There, on my pillow, was a crisp white envelope with my name on it. Traditionally, we stashed love letters on birthdays and anniversaries on each other's pillows.

June 1, 1995

My Dear Cynthia,

My heart is aching. Seeing you so sad, day after day, is so very difficult. I want to be a source of strength and a vision of the future for us yet your sorrow, like an ocean overtaking the shore, washes up on me and saps me of the very strength I need to have for you, for Bobby, for us. Intellectually I know it is time that will help us stem this tide. But neither time nor anything else will bring our sweet Samantha home. Nothing will stop the pain. But somehow we must find a place for her in our hearts without losing the time we need for each other and for Bobby. I need you sweetheart.

I love you dearly, - Neal

I walked back to the kitchen and wiped my eyes, trying not to cry. Neal turned off the television and stood up to hold me.

"I love you so much. So much. I want to see you smile again," he said.

The tears came pouring down my cheeks.

"I'm sorry. I wish I knew a different way to be, but right now... you know how much I love you, don't you?" I said.

Part of me envied Neal, going back to work, having a place to hang his hat other than home. Routine worked well for him. I tried to establish some routine, too, but wasn't nearly as successful. In marriage, we'd been in sync on many things but grief was not one of them.

"I'm just afraid," he said, "you'll become so rooted in the stage you're in, that you'll think I'm being terribly insensitive and we'll never be standing on common ground again." It was a legitimate fear.

June 2, 1995

My Sweet Samantha,

I'm dying. I'm sure of it. This week has been endless and it's only Wednesday. Over Memorial Day we went to the cemetery to pick out a marker. A marker! Oh my God. I should be picking out your dresses. Will I ever be able to stand Wednesdays again?

Love, Mom

I was having a challenging day; the strain of returning to the cemetery pulled me pretty low. It's never a smart thing to get into the car and drive while you're feeling distraught. Fortunately, nothing bad happened. Not this time. While Bobby took his afternoon nap, I got in my car and on a whim, I headed west toward the beach. As I glided down West Channel Road and could see the ocean before me, I veered north down Pacific Coast Highway, away from home. The waves hitting the shore had a hypnotic rhythm, soothing as a lullaby. I turned the radio off and rolled down the windows. The wind stirred up loose tissues from the dash and they blew around the car like a snow flurry. My car surged forward as I goosed the accelerator and if the stoplight at Topanga and Pacific Coast Highway hadn't flashed red, I could've glided up north to the Ventura County line or beyond. To say I wasn't grounded would've been gross understatement. The vacant parking lot opened its arms to me and I embraced it.

Topanga State Beach is a surfer's beach; the shoreline is too rocky and exposed to be very inviting to anyone else. A thick layer of fog drooped over the beach like a canopy and I was drawn to it. The edge of Pacific Coast Highway was dotted with beat-up cars with perfectly waxed boards secured to their roofs. I seemed to be the only idiot paying for parking. I longed to pull the heavy fog over me like a blanket.

The view from the top of the concrete stairs allowed me to scan the shoreline. I saw no traces of young moms with children, no young lovers making out on their towels. In the distance were about two-dozen surfers with the singular purpose of reading and riding the right ones. I headed down the stairs and brushed arms with a suntanned beauty with an angled jaw and the signature defined shoulders from daily paddling. "Excuse me," I muttered. He passed me, remote and silent, behind his Maui Jim sunglasses.

Below, on the sand, I passed a group of young men who were struggling to pull their wetsuits up. Graceful and athletic, they tiptoed through the rocks with their boards held firmly under one arm. As they splashed into deeper water they slid their boards in front of them and mounted them in one seamless motion. They paddled further and further from shore, their bodies growing more distant until all I could see was their silhouette against the horizon.

Like a flock of seagulls, they bobbled on the silvery surface. They were as featureless as the water itself but they were musical in the rhythm of the ocean. They waited.

I waited, too. I was mesmerized by the floating image before me. Somehow this random group of guys took on more meaning as a group than they did individually. Their purpose became clear as a wave took form. In an etiquette I didn't understand, a few of them turned their boards away from the horizon and back toward the shore. As the wave grew taller and closer, they were on their knees and a fraction of a second later, on their feet, arms outstretched. The others sat on their boards and watched, as I did, as the ones atop their boards came barreling toward the sand. Some of them did not last long and they dove into the sea that had turned to browns, grays and pale green like a rare mineral. Tethered at the ankle to their surfboards, they soon paddled back out to join the ones they'd left behind. One or two made their ride last long enough for them to carve in and out of the wave, painting a white wake, moving out of the black and white silhouette and into flesh and blood again. As the wave delivered them to shallow water, they hopped off their boards and slipped into the sea. They were close enough for me to make out their wet, darkened hair and their bare, tanned feet. While I expected to see exhilaration in their eyes, they held instead, an expression of quiet satisfaction.

I picked my way around rocks and seaweed. The air smelled salty-clean and the sand felt cool and soft against my feet. The ocean drowned out the sound of the cars on Pacific Coast Highway with its pounding cycle. If I closed my eyes, I could be on any beach on the globe. When I got to the end of the beach and stood below a bank of rocks, I turned around and headed back toward the lifeguard station at the other end. Holding my sneakers high in one hand, I waded out to my knees in the chilly surf and sucked in my breath as the water washed up against my legs. Goose bumps rose along my thighs and arms. I backed out of the ocean and began a quick stride along the firmer sand. The sun began to burn away the marine-layer and the entire ocean transformed from silvery gray to brilliant blue. The horizon opened up before me and I felt a lightness tinge my body as if the sun were a magic wand burning away the gloom I had been clutching about me like a gothic cloak. As I strode up the shoreline I collected little colored glints of sea glass, marveling at the clear, green, brown and blue colors, softened from something menacing to pleasing.

Bob Marley's "One Love" played on the radio as I drove home. The temperature rose and I rolled down all the windows for the cooling breeze. A layer of salt lingered on my skin and I wore it like it was Chanel No. 5.

At the end of the day I discovered the sea glass in my pocket. The faint salty smell brought me to the sound of the surf booming against the shore and the feel of the grainy sand between my toes. The muted skies filtering grayish-gold light one day and brilliantly cloudless blues another, seduced me back again and again.

CHAPTER 10:

THE SYMPATHY CLUB

June 7, 1995

My Sweet Samantha,

One month has managed to creep by since I lost you. I need to be strong today…your Dad called from the office. A friend of his just had a baby and hearing the news was difficult for him. He's been so wonderful to me…I want to be there for him.

These past few weeks I've tried to keep myself busy, though I can truly say you are in my thoughts always, no matter how much I do or don't do. Yesterday and today I spent the mornings with your brother at the beach. His happiness does make me feel better, less sad. Your Grandma Nan keeps telling me not to cry my heart out, that you are in me still, and that you wouldn't want me to be so sad. What can I tell you, sweetheart? I don't buy it that we weren't meant to be together.

Love, Mom

My Mom knew I'd been going to the beach so she invited me out to lunch in the Marina Del Rey, where Neal and I had lived on the peninsula before moving to Beverly Hills. Sitting at an outdoor café on busy Washington Boulevard held little in common with the solitude of Topanga, other than the fact that both flanked the ocean. With its restaurants, bike rentals, and coffee houses, the Marina was thumping with life. We watched roller bladers and bike riders glide by. A few homeless men, eyes locked to the ground, skirted to Speedway, the alley running parallel to the beach. Neither of us hungry, Mom and I picked at our lunches.

"Do you want to take a walk?" Mom asked.

No sooner had we begun our walk when my Mom complained, "I'm wearing the wrong shoes for this."

"You can shake them out when we get back to the car. It's good exercise, walking."

"When you're feeling better, you ought to take a few golf lessons. You were getting pretty good before you had to stop playing...." She stopped herself.

"I don't know."

"It's such a great couple's game. I could baby-sit Bobby while you and Neal played nine holes on a Sunday."

I sighed.

"Did you hear that?" I said.

"What?"

"The sigh. I'm doing it all the time."

"Naturally."

"My heart feels so heavy, no matter how deeply I inhale, I never feel like I've got enough air."

"Try not to."

"Try not to what?"

"To sigh."

We walked all the way down to the jetty where I used to take Bobby in his stroller, rain or shine. Sailboats and motorboats glided in line, moving out of the sheltered harbor to open sea. Like the boats they were on, the people were always busy, always moving. There was a beauty in their purpose. Closer to us, a few people were fishing right off the jetty. Mom was quiet.

"You ready to turn around?" I asked her.

"Your Dad and I are really glad you don't live down here anymore."

"Why?"

"It's just that we feel really blessed to have you so close to us."

"I'm glad, too, Mom."

Soon after my Mom dropped me off at home, Hayley came over with some homemade butternut soup. "Your soups are the best." I placed the Tupperware in the refrigerator and filled a teakettle with water. Bobby came to play with his Kermit puppet with us.

"How was the Marina?" Hayley asked.

"Hasn't changed."

She cleared her throat. "You know I saw Dr. Starre for my check-up today."

"Really?"

"Is it okay to talk about him? I mean, it must remind you of…"

"Everything reminds me, but it's okay. I have my check-up with him in a couple days."

"He feels so bad. It sounds crazy, but Greg and I think if you ended up staying with him, it wouldn't be such a bad thing. You'd get the best care anywhere when you get pregnant again."

"Whoa. Let's not get ahead of ourselves."

"Yeah, but you are going to try?"

A mental picture of Neal and I turned away from each other in bed came to mind.

"Aren't you?" She looked at me funny.

"Maybe. I don't know."

"Why not?"

"The autopsy still hasn't arrived. Sorry, but can we talk about this later?"

Hayley wasn't the only one posing questions about another baby. A few days later Rachel and her husband came to visit me. Even though we were close as sisters and had helped each other through the hard times, at that moment I felt like we were worlds apart. Grieving wasn't something I knew how to share. Didn't want to know, either.

"I have to come see you, Rodya. Even if it's only a short visit," Rachel said on the phone.

Her husband and Neal went out to the backyard and sat in the shade, drinking beers while Rachel and I sat next to one another on the couch. I looked down and saw her slim muscular thighs beside my own which still looked puffy by comparison. I still had more weight to shed from the pregnancy.

"Promise me we're not going to sit here in my den and cry for two hours, okay?" I asked.

"Deal," she said. "How are you feeling? You look good."

"Don't believe your lying eyes," I tried for a smile. "How are the sailing classes going?" Her husband was an avid sailor and she was game to join him.

"You wouldn't believe how much math is involved," she said, "I thought it was going to be all fun and games."

"It could be worse; you could've married a guy into climbing Everest."

"Really, Cyn. How are you?"

"There are some good days and there are still plenty of bad ones. Problem is, I'm not much use at predicting what's in store." Being on our best behavior drove us both nuts; we sat there, quiet, unsure what to say. Through the French doors, I watched Neal and Rachel's husband swing Bobby on the tree swing. I scratched my head, "We've scared the men off. Maybe we ought to invite them in, out of the sun." I started to rise from the couch.

"Can I ask you something, Rodya?"

I sat back down. "Sure."

"You're going to get pregnant again, right? Maybe we'll time it so we can go through it together."

"Correct me if I'm wrong, but don't you need to be having sex to make a baby?"

A little chuckle escaped her. "I want to be there for you, Rodya."

"I miss Samantha too much. It's only been a month. I just..." I saw the tears in her eyes and I stopped. It was awful to be me. "So? You guys are thinking about having a baby." I tried to sound myself, to smile and quietly change the subject away from me.

The "are you going to get pregnant" question popped up again with my old friend Jake who prodded me into having lunch out with him.

Over the years, we had turned to each other in a genuine friendship that rose beyond the guy-girl thing. It had always been, and still is, a friend-friend thing. He taught me to drive stick shift, helped me secure a fake I.D., downed pitchers of margaritas with me our senior year of high school. After two years at Berkeley, he transferred to the University of Southern California and lived a block away from my sorority house. We had a shorthand that most boyfriends had no way to live up to. Sucking down too many tequila shots one evening, he heroically carried me to the car and drove me home from Glendale, stopping every five minutes so I could catch my breath - and not puke all over his car.

We were seated at a table for two in the bright, overly air-conditioned *Daily Grill*, looking over the menus. I felt his eyes on me and when I looked up, he was staring at my neck where my new silver "baby" charms were dangling. One was a boy, "Bobby" engraved on the surface, and the other was a girl, "Samantha".

"Don't you think it makes people uncomfortable to see that?" Jake asked.

"Does it make you uncomfortable?"

"Well, yeah. It does."

I looked across the restaurant.

"Look, Jake. She was my kid. I don't want to hide that from the world."

"But it's not like you knew her," he said, gentle as a chef's knife slicing clean through me.

"You couldn't be further from the truth. Don't get me wrong but maybe since you guys don't have a kid yet, you don't understand how much I did know her and love her."

"I don't mean to sound like a jerk or anything but you *do* have a kid. And you can have lots more if you want to."

"You're missing the point. You don't substitute one baby for another."

"I'm sorry. I don't exactly get it but I love you."

"And I love you."

His eyes moved past me but he wasn't looking at anything in particular.

"Neal must know a lot of good lawyers but if not, I can recommend a couple guys through my office."

"Who says we're suing him?"

"From what you said…it just seemed like it was kind of his fault."

It was futile to explain to Jake how in many ways, I still thought of Dr. Starre as a friend.

After work, Neal came home and was sifting through the mail. Everyday since we lost Samantha, there were sympathy cards flooding the mailbox. "God works in mysterious ways", "We're holding our children closer and dearer because of what's happened to you", "I know death can cause friendships to die, too."

"Jake sends his regards. I saw him for lunch."

"How is he?" Neal asked.

"He's doing okay. Thinks we should be suing Dr. Starre. I bet most people feel that way."

Neal handed me a card. "Read this one. It's kind of pretty," he said, holding up one in particular.

"We got that one last week from somebody."

"Oh. Well I thought it had a nice sentiment."

"Honey, I've seen just about every sympathy card they've got out on the market. Don't they make you kind of sick?"

"People mean well. They really do."

"It's infuriating to be the subject of someone's sympathy. I can't get used to it."

"No one knows what to say," he shrugged.

"I know, I know."

While I had the luxury to keep people at bay and keep my demons to myself, Neal was out in the 'real world'. Though he was devastated by the loss, he was used to keeping his emotions in check, his reactions cool and controlled, in the executive suite. With all my snarling and clawing at the world, sometimes I felt more like a feral cat than a wife when standing in the same room with Neal.

At some point, I kept a few cards tied together with a big rubber band. They stood like a Rosetta Stone; in case I ever needed to re-visit this period in history, I'd have a kind of artifact to translate the incomprehensible.

My frustration mounted as I'd check the mail at three o'clock and find piles of sympathy cards and no autopsy report. My persistent calls to the pathology department at Westside Regional Hospital earned me only vague responses like; "They ought to send it out pretty soon." I clung onto my goal of finding out "why" like a drowning man clings to a piece of driftwood.

The next time I saw Dr. Starre I vowed to seek his help in getting the autopsy.

CHAPTER 11:

BEFORE AND AFTER

June 10, 1995

My Sweet Samantha,

This morning I saw Dr. Starre for my one month check up and I realize I've had a lot of anxiety about whether I would continue seeing him for my care. We spent an hour in his office, mostly talking. I see the deep compassion he has for us; he shared with me some of the difficulties he's had in his own personal life. I can't ever say what life would be like today had he induced labor on the night I came to see him but that's not worth talking about now. We are where we are. I want to move past placing blame and feeling anger. I may never know why you had to die so soon. Dr. Starre wanted me to think about the next pregnancy. How can I? My head is filled with thoughts of you.

Love, Mom

Walking back through the door into Dr. Starre's office wasn't easy. The simple act of driving past it on my way to the bank or pharmacy made me shudder. According to the digital clock on Neal's nightstand I was already ten minutes late. I fussed with my hair and changed my shirt a couple of times. Who could say whether it was stalling or some idiotic notion of looking good?

It was a Saturday and Dr. Starre came in especially for me on his day off. He wore a cable v-neck tennis sweater and I imagined he'd just finished his game and made his way to me. During the examination, there would be no polite nurse standing in the corner of the room for etiquette's sake. "How are you doing?" he asked.

"Alright," I said too quietly.

"Alive," he repeated, not having quite heard what I said.

Since he admitted his fault to me in the hospital room at Westside Regional, we hadn't been alone together. This was our last chance to get past the doctor/patient protocol and move into the realm of lifelong friends that only a shared disaster could have brought about. I was ready to shed the awkwardness of our phone calls and the nervousness of seeing him again.

He guided me to an examining room where a paper jacket and sheet were waiting for me on the table. "I'll be back in a couple of minutes." He left, closing the door behind him.

Standing there, I exhaled and took in the room. The table, the lamp, the wallpaper, looked familiar. And yet, it was strange territory. Then I realized he might walk in, just as I was pulling my panties past my ankles; an astonishingly wrong thing to have happen. Quickly, I set about pulling off my clothes. I wrapped the paper jacket on top, a sheet over my lap. It seemed to take quite a while for his return. When he finally did gently knock on the closed door and come back in he had his white doctor's gown on, pulled so snugly over his thick, cotton sweater, it was unintentionally hilarious.

I began to seriously wonder if the goal of lifelong friends was realistic when we were barely able to play the roles of doctor and patient. Without other patients and staff people in the office, the room was quiet to the point of eerie. Like any other gynecological exam, I sat back and raised my legs into the stirrups. This time, however, I felt even more self-conscious than usual.

"Everything looks fine," he cleared his throat, "after you get dressed, meet me in my office."

A few minutes later I was seated across the desk from Dr. Starre. His desk and chair were Pottery Barn catalog type furniture, painted to look like old American pieces though they were probably manufactured recently in China. There were an odd assortment of knick-knacks – a miniature plug-in water fountain, a pointed stem suspended over sand, which randomly drew abstract shapes and some black and white photos of his family.

"You can do anything you want to do now. Anything. Sex is okay." Like that was the first thing on my mind. I took a deep breath.

"So I can hike in the hills and all that."

"Oh, yeah. And after a couple of normal periods, you can get pregnant again."

I didn't have anything to say to him.

He continued, "It would make you feel better."

"No. I think it would make *you* feel better." I shifted in the chair, uncomfortable.

"It's up to you but if you never got pregnant again it's like your life would have stopped right here. You'd never know what it would have been like with more children."

"I'm not anywhere close to what I'd call ready."

"It's like the accident I had. For a while, every time I got back on my bike, I felt like a truck was going to side-swipe me again. It was terrifying."

"Well, obviously the thought has crossed my mind that I could lose another baby."

"I have to tell you, I'm fairly certain that won't be the case." He paused a moment. "Another thing that ought to give you some peace of mind is: None of this was your or Neal's fault. I mean, we have friends who inadvertently forgot to strap their baby into the stroller. He was strangled to death. They're out of their minds with grief."

"Oh my God," I muttered.

"It's kind of strange, I guess, but each new child I have, I seem to love them all more deeply."

Most of my friends supported Dr. Starre's views about getting pregnant right away. My hope was to find a place for Samantha in my life and in my heart. I couldn't possibly think about having another child until I came to peace with her death.

"If you want to blame someone, blame me. If I'd taken you into the hospital that night...if I'd taken an ultrasound...." he cleared his throat.

"You did what you thought was best. What else can I say?" There was an awkward silence. He toyed with a brass paperweight on his desk.

"I'm going to have you screened for lupus in case that had any bearing on what happened."

I sat up at attention. "Do you think that's why I lost her?"

"I just want to rule it out, really."

I slumped back down.

"It's torture waiting for the autopsy. Do you think you can put some pressure on the hospital?"

"Of course. I'll call on Monday."

Dr. Starre walked me to my car and my knees felt rubbery like I'd been on a Ferris wheel all afternoon. Maybe he sensed something. Maybe he didn't.

"I'll keep the letter you sent me forever," he said. When he hugged me goodbye, he hugged me hard and did not let go for a long time.

The next day Rabbi Stern stopped by with a grocery bag full of toys for Bobby and Kona coffee for Neal and I. "How are you doing?" he asked.

"Okay."

"Your Mom and Dad?"

"They're taking it tough. Especially my Mom."

"Is there anything I can do to help?" he asked.

"Actually, I've been wondering: Do you know of anyone else in the congregation I could talk to? Someone who's had a stillborn?"

"Well, I'll have to think about it. I don't remember anyone, offhand."

"There must be someone over the years, right? I mean last night I read an article that said somewhere between one in two hundred and fifty women and one in five hundred women suffers having a stillborn."

"Can I call you tomorrow? Let me make some inquiries."

The next day he called with two phone numbers. Eager to find a role model, I called Michaela. She was happy. Too happy.

"Let me see. It was about three years ago. I think. Or was it four? I got pregnant again right away with my daughter."

I was floored. "Did you worry? About something going wrong again?"

"Not at all."

"Are you serious?"

"God would never let that happen to me again! He wouldn't give me more than I could handle."

Another call. This one to Edie. Her voice was surprised but pleased to have someone to talk to. It'd been a year since they'd lost the baby. The smell of pain was sharp enough to detect over the phone. Her doctor told her in the delivery room that, "This is not a viable fetus." She sheepishly confided that she hadn't gone to bed with her husband in a long time. Her body still looked like she was five months pregnant and she knew she should be trying to do something about it but she couldn't get motivated.

"How about a walk around the block? Just putting one foot in front of the other helps me," I said.

I was grateful to talk to these women but they didn't exactly fill me with confidence that I was ever going to be the same or even close to the person I'd been before.

And then Neal remembered a business associate whose wife, Michelle, had given birth to a baby that had died eight years earlier.

"When I'm talking to you, it's so weird. It's like it all happened yesterday," Michelle said.

"Thank you so much for sharing all this with me. I know it's not easy."

"Like you, it was all so unexpected. When I finally got pregnant again…and we waited several years…I felt so blessed to have Xander. He is so special to me."

"I'm sure."

"With my daughter, I weaned her off the breast when she was ten months old. I'm still breastfeeding Xander and he turned two last month."

"Wow."

"It's a comfort thing. You know, we just do it at night."

I was Goldilocks from "The Three Bears" searching for someone "just right" to talk to. Neal and I discussed the bereaved moms' reactions to their loss. Some moved on at break-neck pace, while others seemed totally mired in one place.

"What about group therapy?" I asked Neal.

"Ugh. Do we really want to share this in front of a group of strangers?"

"Well, if it helps us feel better."

"Cyn, I gotta tell you, at least for me, I don't think it would make me feel better. But if you want to go, I'll go."

Not convinced that group therapy *was* for us, I found out from Hayley about one of her best buddies. Lily was a neonatal nurse in San Diego who had a stillborn. When we got on the phone I could've cried in relief. She'd made it. She was whole. She'd waited a couple of years before getting pregnant again; her toddler was healthy and her pregnancy uneventful. She had a job she was good at. The telltale barometer of her healing was her sense of humor. Hours on the phone passed like seconds.

"Whoops. Should've put you on hold there," she said.

"What?"

"My kid's going through toilet training so we've got the diaper off him when we're at home."

"Oh, yeah. We're still working on that with Bobby, too."

"How exactly do you get a urine stain out of the Berber carpet?"

"Oh, no." I laughed.

"It's amazing how it all comes back so fresh. I'll tell you something. It does not seem like five years have passed. You guys going to any support groups?"

Taking Lily's advice, I signed Neal and I up for a bereaved parents support group that met monthly at Westside Regional Hospital. Neal was skeptical; being there meant leaving work early and sharing a private tragedy in public. It didn't help that the door to the room was locked and the facilitator, a smartly dressed woman in her forties, had no key. She had us try another room. Locked. We backtracked down the dim hallway and searched for a custodian to open a room for us. Neal checked his watch and took a deep breath. Finally, the custodian showed up and unlocked the room. We filed in and the facilitator suggested we move the seats into a circle.

One pretty Latin girl, barely twenty, was seated next to her boyfriend. He looked about as enthusiastic as my husband about being there. None of the men were speaking up.

"A year ago my baby died. I keep her picture with all my family photos. My boyfriend," she turned to the young man beside her, "he doesn't really like to see it there. I wanted to die after the baby died. I'm so sad all the time. Sometimes I still think about killing myself."

I stole a glance at Neal and saw his clenched jaw was a warning; he was not happy about being there.

A single mom from Jamaica spoke next. "I don't know what happened. I don't know why my baby died."

My stomach lurched, terrified for her. I was *still* waiting for the autopsy. My fear was that I'd end up like this lost woman, clueless as to why I'd lost my baby.

The facilitator looked visibly upset but tried to compose herself.

The woman continued. "My neighbors say I am at fault because I smoked a few times. Marijuana."

"What did your doctor say?" the facilitator asked.

"The baby's head was too big."

"Was it anencephaly? Is that what the doctor said?"

"I smoked marijuana only four times. I don't think that hurt the baby."

The zip code, clothing brands, and skin color faded in that room. We were sisters who knew first hand what it was like to know the dreams you had for your child were never coming true. Instinctively, we knew another baby wouldn't take the place of the one we'd lost. No one said it out loud that night but it was clear our lives could now be defined as "before the baby died" and "after".

Chapter 12:

On a Good Day

June 28, 1995

Sweet Samantha,

I've embarked on a new journey. I'm writing a book about you. It's a story of how all of us grew to love you and it's about hope – looking forward – and knowing you will always be a part of us. I've come to see you all around me; whenever there's beauty, grace and mystery, you are there. When I think of the innocence of my childhood, all those happy times, I think of being outdoors. Hiking in the mountains with my Dad and Greg. Riding horses in the dry, dusky heat at summer camp. Holding my Mom's hand as we floated in the ocean in Hawaii. When I see something of beauty around me, I think of you.

Love, Mom

My progress was like a drunk's gait.

"You're back," I'd tell myself, and I actually believed it. Unfortunately, it took very little for me to lurch one way or the other; even change direction completely, if any little thing caught me off guard. On a "good" day, I was skipping forward, feeling invincible. My goal - New Levis. My destination - Fred Segal's on Melrose. A Hefty trash bag filled with maternity clothes made an arc as I hoisted it into my trunk to give away to Goodwill.

It was the beginning of summer vacation, and teenagers in suggestive, ripped jeans and funky Doc Marten boots were window shopping the boutiques and sipping lattes at the coffee houses. Fred Segal's was a hip series of boutiques selling everything from vintage Levis to high-end cosmetics to organic coffee. Out of nowhere, I heard a voice behind me. I turned around. It was a lanky salesman with unnaturally black hair.

"Can I help you find something?"

"Looking for a pair of 501's, please."

His next question, innocent as it was, threw me for a loop: "What size?"

"Umm. I don't know exactly." The clerk looked befuddled.

"What do you usually wear?"

"A 29 or 30 but I had a baby recently and…"

The clerk perked up, "Boy or girl?"

I hesitated and the clerk gave me a funny look.

"Girl."

"What's her name?"

This was going nowhere fast and the inspiration to do something frivolous and fun was fizzling away faster than bubbles in a flute of champagne.

"Look, I don't mean to be rude but I don't have a whole lot of time."

"Of course. You need to get back to the baby! All right. What kind of wash do you prefer? We have a new vintage denim."

"Anything in a 32, please."

Moving quickly, I hid behind the curtain of the changing room and took the first pair he offered me. I pulled off my Adidas tennis shoes and slipped out of the elasticized maternity shorts. My image in the mirror was decidedly unhip. The clerk slung four pairs of jeans over the dresser door. The first pair I tried fit too loosely in the behind but I didn't bother with the others. I swept back up to the cash register and plunked down my credit card, hoping to distract the clerk from asking any more questions.

Outside, the mid-morning sun was hot and wonderful against my skin; I didn't want to go home to a bunch of sympathy cards and calls. A guilty pleasure of having free time washed over me. My tongue ran across my lips and I thought about how good a cold beer would taste. I hung a lazy arm out the window to signal my left turn onto Melrose. The shoe stores, used clothing boutiques and record stores were a colorful collage in motion. At a stoplight, I sensed someone staring at me. Next to me, a guy in a new F150 truck caught my eye. He had a hangdog smile on his face. I flashed him a brazen smile right back. Sleeping with a stranger sounded good right about then.

At night, my mind took me places without my even needing the car, without my even being conscious. Without my permission.

Loud music, cheap sofa and plenty of beer. It looked like the kind of rental house a handful of students lives in. It was already dark and the new moon was high in the sky when I strolled in, heels clicking, mini-skirt swishing. It wasn't chilly out but I shivered a little in the night air. Someone handed me a plastic tumbler filled with foamy beer.

All my film school buddies were there. My funny production partner Pete. My co-editor, Burt. Talented Dave who I dated on and off. Even shy Matt, the cinematographer who shot my last film. We were laughing deep and hard. The beer was cold and tasty but when I looked back up, the front door was gone. A wall was in its place. My eyes slowly adjusted to my surroundings. The people I'd shared such good times with were in fact, vampires. Their skin was pale and their teeth had pointy edges.

Bedtime was no longer something I looked forward to. Poor Neal got rattled as I'd wake with a start. He'd prop himself on one elbow, "Are you okay?"

"Yes. Go back to sleep."

Still, I'd throw on a robe and sweep down the hallway to Bobby's room. Just in case. Just in case something inexplicable had gone wrong. He was always there in his new twin bed, cozy, breathing, and safe.

Then I'd be like a sentry, searching the quiet corners of every room in the house for the boogey man. My last stop was my own closet. Half-asleep, I flicked on the closet light, as I fanned my hand through the clothes. When my eyes adjusted to the light, I realized my hand was resting on the new Levis, hanging on the rack - cold evidence the day was real, the nightmare a fantasy.

The nightmares continued for about a year. And each time I had one, I had to pry the dream from the reality. I had to convince myself all over again that my little boy was sleeping even though my demons were wide awake.

CHAPTER 13:

HAPPY TRAILS

The next day I was back in a closet; this time it was in the lemony-yellow room I had been avoiding every time I walked down the hall to Bobby's room. Tiny pink dresses and velour onesies were breaking our hearts. Neal and I got to work folding clothes and storing them in bags. I stripped the bedding off the crib and began to fold them, too. We gathered an armful of stuffed animals into a pile on the floor. The phone rang and I left the room, grateful for a break, to answer it.

"It's your friend, Annie! How are you and the baby doing?"

Annie was a talented writer I'd hired for a NBC project that year. We'd spent a lot of time working out the story and hadn't had much time outside the office. Though I liked her very much, she was a new friend and I hadn't thought to call her with the bad news.

"The baby didn't make it Annie. She died."

"Oh my God. What happened?"

"We think it was a cord accident. I'm still waiting for the autopsy."

"Around her neck?"

"No. It was just wound around itself. Like a garden hose."

"My God. I'm so sorry, Cynthia. Are you up for a visitor?"

I hedged. "Maybe later."

"When?"

"Umm," I stalled.

"What are you doing this afternoon?"

Annie wasn't about to be put off, to my surprise.

"Well, maybe just for a little while."

"How's Neal doing?" she asked.

Most of my friends barely asked about him and I was really touched she did.

"He's dealing with it the best he can."

"I'll see you this afternoon."

Neal's voice pulled me away.

"Cynthia?"

"I'll catch you later, Annie." I hung up and looked up at him; his arms were crossed and his mouth was a little minus sign.

"What?" I said.

"How could you leave me like that?"

"Like what?"

"This is killing me and you left me all alone with it." He gestured off down the hallway.

"I'm sorry. The phone." I shrugged.

"Well couldn't you tell me that you'd be awhile?"

"I was only on a couple minutes."

"That's not true."

I snapped back, "Why didn't you just stop doing what you were doing?"

"Because we said we were doing this today." He said each word lethal as a rat trap tripped against my neck, snapping me in two.

"I wanted to talk with her."

"You just left me hanging there. Jesus."

"Leave it. I'll handle the rest myself, okay?"

His mouth fell open like he was about to say something else but I didn't give him a chance. I rushed past him out the screen doors to the yard. The air had been sucked out of the room and I was choking. I took deep breaths, trying to calm down. The sound of water drew my attention. Our gardener, Daniel, was watering azaleas. How much had he heard? He gave the hose a twist and the water abruptly shut off; the image was unsettling. From the pained look on his face, I could see he'd overheard us. He walked a few steps toward me.

"Como estas, Senora?"

"No se, Don Daniel. No se." The "Don" was a sign of respect.

Thoughtful, he pulled at a few weeds. I stared stupidly at the hose under pressure in his hands.

"Estaba embarazada mi esposa. Con gemelos. Twins. They died before they were born."

I looked up at him.

"I'm so sorry. Lo siento."

"She was angry. Yelling at me all the time. I never knew what to say, you know?"

I threw a look over my shoulder. The den was empty and I didn't know where Neal was.

"You know what my grandfather used to say about marriage?" I said.

"What?"

"The first hundred years are the hardest."

Annie had suggested we take a short hike at Tree People Park, located in the Santa Monica mountains, off of Coldwater Canyon. Named for the streambeds, which ran heavily during rainy season, Coldwater Canyon is now a busy street connecting Beverly Hills to Sherman Oaks and other parts of the San Fernando Valley. In 1910, however, it was a quiet, dirt road flanked by bean fields, which, after threshing, were available to anyone who cared to pick beans.

After my earlier spat with Neal, I felt like I couldn't breathe in the same house. With all the pain I was dealing with, I just couldn't handle any tension with him. Any reserves of strength I possessed were being bestowed upon Bobby.

"I'm going hiking with Annie."

"When do you think you'll be back?"

"Not sure. Two hours, maybe. If you have any errands you want to do, go ahead. The babysitter's here until four."

He raised his eyebrows as I skipped out the door to join Annie who was waiting for me in the driveway in her Volvo station wagon. I made baby talk to her standard poodle Tucker who rode in back. He was too cool and macho to respond much to my cooing.

The park was only a few miles north. The seventies style lettering on their "Tree People" sign gave me the impression it would be a puny section of the state park. My expectations were pretty low even though Annie had been raving about it. Baseball hat slung low over my face; I hoped not to run into anyone I knew. We wandered down a shady path of broken bark and twigs that led to a brief, narrow incline down to the trail. Almost immediately, I was taken aback at the view. It was green and lush with a few low-key ranch homes hidden among the trees in the distance. Further away, toward Laurel Canyon, I recognized the Mt. Olympus gated community and beyond that, the San Bernardino Mountains. It was a pocket of beauty nestled between bustling Beverly Hills and frantic Studio City.

As we started up a steep hill, our talk slowed down. We wandered onto deer trails and found life aplenty; dun colored rabbits and mountain squirrels that were wiry and smaller than the ones in town.

"Thank you for coming out with Tucker and me."

"I owe you the thanks, Annie. This place is great. And you. You are so easy to be with."

When I got home, I shared my experience of the hike with Neal and he was open to going up there with me. The spat was pretty much forgotten. It wasn't important anymore. I was feeling good and Neal was relieved to see that side of me again.

In time, I made Tree People my own, as have many others looking for some quiet. Weekends were crowded but when I drove up there mid-week, my friends were hawks suspended high on the wind, circling, keeping watch over the woods. My other friends, the Blue Jays, flitted around the brush, scouting for beetles and lizards, sounding much larger than they were. The dangerous ones made no sound at all - the rattlers - until you were already in their face. Something about the pungent citrus smell of the eucalyptus with their pale, smooth bark awakened my energy. The ever-changing life there, and me, solid in the middle of it - no more or less important than anything else on the trail - was a gift.

CHAPTER 14:

UNANSWERED PRAYERS

July 20, 1995

Sweet Samantha,

    The summer is finally beginning to look and smell like summer. Bobby & I play together in the pool and my skin is browning from my hikes and afternoons in the water. The time I'm alone is what keeps me sane, I think. My mind wanders and I swear I can feel you near me somehow. My eyes have changed; I don't see things the way I used to. I see more, for one thing. I see more clearly, for another. This morning the sunlight was coursing through the branches of the Elm trees and as beautiful as it was, it almost hurt to see it.

    My book is taking shape. I realize part of my work now is also laying tracks from opposite ends of the map because your Dad and I were sent crashing apart when we lost you. If we keep working at it, I know we will be joined and whole again.

    Dr. Starre was over today, trying to shed light on what took you from us. I'm sorry to say, the circumstances are still very shaded to me. No explanation makes any sense.

    Love, Mom

The hinge on our squeaky brass mail slot alerted me to the mail delivery and I would always rush out to see if the autopsy had arrived. Over eight weeks had passed since I signed off on having the procedure done. This afternoon, among the sympathy cards and bills, stood the gray manila envelope with the Westside Regional Hospital return address stamped in the corner.

First thing, I called Neal. Next, I snuck off to my office in the backhouse, gripping the envelope in my hands like it was a genie in a bottle, ready to grant my wish. Finally, finally, I would know why my baby had died and how.

I sat at my desk and opened the report. As my eyes skimmed through the first couple of pages, I came across words I didn't recognize like "petechiae", "foramen orale", "lobulations" and "corticomedullary". I got down my Webster's Dictionary and started all over. Here is an excerpt:

SUMMARY:

"The mother is a 30 year old, G-2,P-1 who had an uneventful pregnancy until 40 3/7 weeks when intrauterine fetal demise was identified. The cause of the intrauterine fetal demise was thought to be due to a cord accident: *pleural petechiae and acute meconium aspiration signify acute distress rather than longstanding placental insufficiency. (*petechiae are tiny reddish spots containing blood that appears in skin or mucous membranes.)

At autopsy, a 3360 gram female infant was received. Grossly, no external or internal anomalies were identified.

Given the unremarkable gross and microscopic findings demonstrating only acute distress in this infant, the cause of death is most probably due to a cord accident as noted by the clinician, there is no evidence of infectious or hereditary etiologies."

I began to feel wobbly and sick to my stomach like I was having motion sickness. Reading the report was worlds away from what I'd expected. The report was filled with language I could barely understand and there was no definitive, 'yes this is why the baby died', kind of statement.

With Webster's Ninth Collegiate Dictionary by my side, I tried to interpret the words I didn't understand. When I came to a word defined as "skin flaking off", I slammed the book shut.

My own interpretation is that Samantha's body seemed to shut down after the cord accident. The rest of it didn't sink in; the statistics of how much her brain weighed, how long she measured crown to rump were meaningless.

The answer to why we had lost Samantha had been the most important piece of the puzzle to me. After two months, I realized the answer depended on who was doing the asking. One mother's answer would be: "It was God's will." Another might say: "It was an accident." Still another might say: "It was all my fault".

Neal's answer was: "This happened because our next child had to be brought into the world for some reason we may never fully understand." Less emotional than I was, or maybe just better at holding his emotion in check, Neal read the autopsy and saw the positive in it: There didn't seem to be any physiological reason not to get pregnant again if we decided to go down that path.

My Dad who is a retired dentist, wanted to see the report. When he came by to pick it up, he stood in the threshold of the kitchen door and grasped my shoulders in his large hands. Looking straight into my eyes he said, "Cindy, you have so many good things in your life...and one terrible thing. Remember the good."

I walked with him down the driveway to his old Chevrolet. He had to go slow, bending over to get in the car. He took a breath before hauling in one leg and then the other. He had worked hard all his life and it took a toll on him physically. His back ached, his hearing was impaired, and he had had a heart attack. Thing is, he never felt sorry for himself and he rarely complained. I had been allowing myself too much self-pity. And as always, when I wiped away the last tear, I was precisely back in the place I'd started. My Dad was right. I had to remember the good.

When the phone rang early Saturday morning, I knew Dr. Starre's voice as soon as he uttered the first syllable of my name. He was making good on his promise to go over the autopsy with us and I was grateful for his making the time for us on his day off and for offering to meet at our house instead of the office. The last time I'd seen him, one month earlier at my four-week check up, I had not made up my mind about having him as my doctor. Neal was anxious to hear what he had to say because he wasn't sure whether or not to pursue things from a legal standpoint. In either case, we were both looking forward to a more concrete and detailed explanation than we could provide ourselves from the technical language of the autopsy.

Arms flying, I scooped up Barney video boxes and picked up bits of French toast that didn't make it to Bobby's mouth so I could have the house in order before Dr. Starre arrived. Wouldn't it be nice to have a dog, I thought? Moving to my bathroom, I quickly brushed my teeth and applied some silvery pink lipstick. I wanted to make a good impression, to look stronger than I really felt. Every encounter with Dr. Starre was an opportunity for me to find answers to what happened and to exchange the kind of solace that only a shared disaster could offer two people.

The babysitter took Bobby for a walk in the stroller so the three of us could have a discussion without interruption. Even after Neal and I had talked to Bobby about the baby being gone, he had not once brought up the subject.

Neal was still in shorts and the day-glow yellow Laker tee shirt he'd slept in the night before. He didn't care if Dr. Starre saw crumbs on the floor or wrinkles in his shirt. All he cared about was getting information.

"Where should we sit with him? Here?" He gestured to the breakfast room table. There were still some dirty dishes in the sink.

I shook my head. "It's beautiful outside. Let's sit under the Jacaranda tree."

Neal took hold of a small round table from the patio and moved it under the shade. I started to pick up the lawn chairs, but he stopped me and carried them himself.

When I escorted Dr. Starre to our backyard, he was wearing a black silk Hawaiian shirt and lightweight slacks. If I could've placed a Mai Tai in his hand, he would've looked like the picture-perfect Southern Californian.

"Your home is great. You guys going swimming later?"

"Maybe," I said. "What are you doing today?"

"I'm so busy during the week; I usually like to do nothing at all. You know, lie in the sun by the pool all weekend with the kids."

A mental picture of Dr. Starre reclined in a lounge chair, reading a novel out by his pool came to mind. In the background were his kids and his wife. I'd heard he lived nearby.

Neal cleared his throat. "So, you read the autopsy?"

Dr. Starre opened the pages of the report and spread them across the table. His muscular, tanned hands spread the pages out, working away the creases, smoothing away the questions. His professional evaluation would put my mind at ease. Dr. Starre looked up from the paper and into my eyes. There it was. In the eyes. He had seen something I had missed, that Neal had overlooked. I clung to his every gesture and word. He looked back into my eyes and I felt certain that he understood me.

"The pathologists came to the same conclusion I did: The baby probably died of a cord accident."

I waited. There had to be more. "Probably" left room the size of Montana for other conclusions.

"You're sure?" I said.

He came over to tell me that? Where were those Barney videos? I wanted to smack him with one.

"Remember when I showed you the cord?"

"Yes."

"There was a notch in it. A small notch."

"Actually, I never saw it." There was an edge in my voice I didn't care for.

"In the hospital, when you were in delivery…"

"What I mean is, I saw the cord but I never did make out the notch when you presented it to me. Though I think I was losing my mind at the time."

Neal sat forward in his chair and took hold of my hand, all the while looking at Dr. Starre. The pressure of his fingers against mine steadied me.

"It was an accident," Neal said in a measured tone. "How often do you see this?"

"Almost never. I've been very lucky."

Looking for a hero, I found Jimmy Buffet, fanning himself with an autopsy report, instead.

CHAPTER 15:

NEW CHAPTER

A very bright friend, whom I respected enormously, once told me, "If you look at the world through your heart you cry, and when you look at it through your head you laugh."

Thumbing randomly through my journal, I wondered if I could tell a story about what had happened to us. There were pages of letters to Samantha and also private musings on my day-to-day life since we'd lost our girl. I had serious reservations about revealing intimate details of my family's life, but I felt inspired to try to put on paper an experience that other moms and their families could find useful and comforting. I remembered how good it felt to talk to Lily and hear how her life was blossoming. My hesitations melted away in the face of the importance of reaching out to others who had not found the right tools to help heal effectively. Sure, I had a long, long way to go but something clicked in me. It may have been having a destination that felt so right.

There were several good writing conferences coming up and I applied to the one that was closest to me in Northern California, The Napa Valley Writers Conference. The deadline to submit material to the conference was only a few weeks away. Every morning I sat at my desk, clicking away at the keyboard, never thinking to check my watch, not once counting the hours to bedtime. I was trying to tell my story, though I was only a couple of months into the grieving process, so that I could share it in a clear and meaningful way. When I'd finished the first twenty-five pages required in the application, I felt like the door had been opened on solitary confinement and I was seeing daylight for the first time in a long while. Annie proofread the pages and I sent the application packet off in the mail.

A few weeks later, when I opened the acceptance letter from the conference, I felt hope. I set about reserving a car and a room. I read books by the authors who were leading panels, like David Shields and Pam Houston. I looked forward to getting solid professional guidance on my work. Best of all, no one at the conference would know or pity me.

In some sense, I took notice that my world had shrunk into the size of a small knot - tight and secret. With something productive to do and something meaningful to offer others, I began to feel some levity again. My goal of writing a book about the loss of my daughter would give meaning to Samantha's life, too. Let's face it, when you read a good memoir, those characters become immortal.

With the writing submission completed, I had some time to hike with Annie again.

"Last time we went for a hike, you said you were ready to go to bed with a stranger."

"I said that?"

"In so many words."

"Come on!" I said.

She raised one eyebrow at me, "Well? Have you and Neal done the deed yet?"

I playfully cuffed her on the head. "Shut up."

"It's perfectly normal to pull back, after what you've been through."

"Normal, huh? And my fantasies about other men?"

"Hmm." She gave me a crooked smile. "Anyone I know?"

"Yeah. Your buddy Denzel."

"Would you ever sleep with him if the opportunity arose?"

"Jesus, Annie!"

"I'm not judging you. It's a question."

"Wouldn't you?" The two of us started laughing. We walked on in silence for a few minutes. She never made me feel like we had to have an on-going dialogue.

"How's the treatment coming?" I asked. She had a writing outline due to present to a studio.

"To tell you the truth, since the eye surgery to correct my vision went south, I don't know if my writing's ever going to be as good as it once was."

"What happened?

"For four years, I've had chronic eye pain. I've been around the country seeing specialists, but nothing's worked."

I hooked an arm around her. "Sorry, Annie."

"How could I complain after what you've been through?"

"Pain is pain," I said. Tucker came crashing out of the brush and we picked the burrs from his wavy, thick fur. "It's something that hurts you. It's real. Who's to say what pain is worse than any other?"

"Still," Annie said, "there's nothing worse than what happened to you."

"No sense in measuring it."

We wound around, climbing up a hillside until the ground leveled off, and we caught our breath. The afternoon was clear and I relished the view of the mountain ranges to the north.

A bout of nerves about whether or not my book would be any good propelled me back up to Tree People a day or two later.

Summer had cooked the leaves from soft, moist green to crisp brown. Every time I came up there, it looked different.

At the trailhead, I noticed a new memorial plaque secured at the base of a young tree. Included with the name, the plaque also listed the dates of birth and death. That somebody had lived over seven decades, and I pictured Samantha's plaque having the same birth and death date. I began to cry at the unfairness of it all. Not pretty girl-tears but big, snotty sloppy ones. Without warning, the toe of my hiking boot snagged a rock and I pitched forward, almost landing on my face. I straightened out and took a deep breath. Gathering myself, I seriously wondered if Samantha was ordering me to quit it.

I blew my nose on my shirtsleeve and shook my head at how stupid I was being. Continuing on, I strode up the side of a mountain, legs pumping, breathing audible. I wanted to get to my "happy place", to grab a handful of mustard plant and watch the yellow buds chalk up my palms. The flight of a hummingbird caught my eye. I stopped to look at it for a couple of minutes and then it flew out of sight. I resumed my hike when I noticed it was back, following me. The creature hovered beside me for a quarter mile. I was considering naming it like a pet when it abruptly rose up and out of sight.

Patience. I wasn't good at waiting for autopsies, calls from Dr. Starre or Neal's moods. Was God trying to teach me patience? I sensed if I could open my eyes a bit wider, see a bigger picture, I would be rewarded with little hummingbirds by my side and happier times.

Patience, however, was as elusive as the hummingbird. Neal drove Bobby and me to Toys R Us to get a new swing for our outdoor tree. Neal didn't buckle his seat belt. I waited a few minutes and he still didn't buckle it. He was listening to a sports update on the radio.

"Honey, buckle up, okay?"

"One sec." He held up one finger.

"Come on!" I said.

"I will," he said. He started to turn the volume up on the baseball scores.

"Dammit. Don't you know by now that bad things can happen to us?"

His eyes flicked to the rearview mirror where he looked at Bobby for a minute. He got that seatbelt on, all right. I stared out the window, sulky, secretly shocked by my own outburst.

"Sorry," I murmured. Though I wasn't sorry at all.

That unhappy mood followed me through to the next morning. I meant to call a dear friend and couldn't recall the number I'd known for years. I sat down to pay bills and had to pull out the newspaper - I couldn't remember the date. I holed up with Bobby, playing games and counting down the days until I could leave for Napa.

How I met Neal is something I wanted to write to Samantha about. Given my testiness earlier in the day, perhaps I needed to refresh my own recollection in the re-telling of our first date.

July 26, 1995

Hi Sweetheart,

Your Dad and I met while working on the same floor of an office building in Century City. He was a business affairs executive for a cable company and I was an assistant to a film producer at a small studio. For one reason or another, I had to cancel on your Dad the first couple times he asked me out. Once it was a friend coming in to see me who'd been out of town. Another time, travel plans with girlfriends conflicted with our arrangements. The less available I was, of course, the more he insisted on seeing me. What I should have been doing the day we finally had our first date was packing, but your Dad was impossible and he refused to wait until I got home at the end of the weekend. All I could manage was an hour with him. To save time, we walked from our offices in Century City to the shopping mall nearby for lemonade. It was Fourth of July weekend and I was going to Mammoth later that evening with girlfriends. The mall wasn't crawling with shoppers the way it is now. Holiday weekend and it looked like a ghost town. For a moment, your Dad and I were the only people in the world. He made me laugh and I found myself confiding in him. In my heart, I knew I could trust him completely. And I'm not going to tell you that his handsome face didn't have an effect on me. As my girlfriends and I drove north to Mammoth later that night, I kept thinking about your Dad and how he made me feel. I was twenty-four years old and had been dating a lot of different guys. He stood out. All it took was a walk to the mall and back, and I was smitten.

We liked Spike Lee films and playing pool and going to museums and going on bike rides and kissing. We could just as easily do nothing but hang out, reading the <u>Sunday Times</u> and smiling over coffee at one another. I knew I wanted to marry him. I'd never been so comfortable with anyone in all my life. He was a lucky charm, too. I became a finalist in the Nicholl Fellowship Screenwriting competition. My boss promoted me to Story Editor. Things were so easy and right. But my Mom was skeptical; he was twelve years my senior, and she pegged him as a lone wolf and career bachelor. Nothing could've been further from the truth.

There have been some more good days but I never thought I would be working so hard at reconstructing my life with Neal, laying track after track, both of us trying to reach each other from opposite sides of the map. Our strength lies in knowing that if we keep hammering away, we will somehow be happy like we used to be when we first looked deep into each other's eyes over glasses of lemonade.

The midsummer light is hard, reflecting off car windshields and sidewalks by ten in the morning. You don't want to leave the house without a baseball cap and sunglasses. Bobby and I swim in the pool each day and my skin is browning from my time spent outdoors. I try to hike or walk each day to keep me sane. The pretty things make me think of you. Orange blossoms. Colorful hummingbirds. Fuchsia rose bushes. Are you watching over us? I love you. You'll always be my girl.

   Love, Mom

CHAPTER 16:

<u>SANCTUARY</u>

J*ournal Entry*
St. Helena, CA   August 1, 1995

> *I'm here in Napa, at Gillwoods, eating a delicious fruit plate and sipping strong, hearty coffee. Beats eating leftover Cheerios. Neal assures me that Bobby is having fun and that everyone at home is doing fine. It's a guilty pleasure to be writing in my journal at a café and to not be responsible for anyone else...*

I kissed Neal goodbye at Los Angeles International airport, on my way to Northern California, to begin my trip to the writer's conference. We were not apart often. When he had business in New York or Europe, I always drove him to the airport, walked to the parking lot and returned home. How odd it felt to watch him turn around, keys in his pocket, heading for the parking lot while I double-checked my own pocket for my boarding pass. As soon as I got on the plane, I checked my purse for the two by two inch pewter frame, which held a photo of Bobby and Neal, wearing matching blue and white pinstriped shirts. The frame had been an "unbirthday" present, a few days earlier from Annie. I looked at it every chance I got.

The plane landed in Oakland and I found the car rental desk, got a map, and finally eased the subcompact car onto the freeway. In the past, I'd traveled with friends and with Neal. This was the first time I had traveled alone. The unfamiliar street names and buildings liberated me like I was a college freshman with my whole life ahead of me. The local radio station played Tom Petty and Mick Jagger and I had to admit that as nervous as I was to leave home, to have my work critiqued, it felt like an adventure.

As I drove along the highway through Napa Valley, there were wineries backed up one after another - St. Supery, Robert Mondavi, Sterling - with tall, decorative iron gates and impressive entrances luring the eye and tempting the palate. The chest-high rows of grape vines with their leafy symmetry had a stillness and logic that soothed me. Behind them, gentle, golden hills bloomed upwards keeping a protective eye on the valley. The muscles in my neck and back that had been seized up without my realizing it, gradually relaxed. The air smelled toasty and clean and awakened an appetite in me I'd lost for months.

Lectures and workshops were held in sunny classrooms at a tiny college campus in St. Helena. At check-in, I made small talk with the college student ahead of me in line and the retired doctor behind me. A feeling of camaraderie began to develop early on. The first day, an outgoing woman set up a dinner for about eight of us at an upscale California cuisine restaurant. From that point on, I hung out with several of these writers and learned most returned to this conference year in and year out.

When I called Neal from my little room at the St. Helena Hotel on Main Street, I had to admit I was having fun. I strolled to a local market and bought fruit and candy to keep in my room. The town was small and charming.

My eyes opened with the sun and I had time before the lectures to get in a good walk. The houses in the area were old but well kept. It was an artsy community with lots of wind chimes and unusually painted craftsman-style homes. Further along, I passed a schoolyard, an old stone church and a school playground. Winding further toward the hills was a small, old cemetery with large moss-covered headstones. The sprinklers were cascading water everywhere and the morning sunlight was caught in the water, shimmering and spinning, sending rainbows over the graves. I expected a jolt in my chest at seeing the image but it never came.

I kept winding higher, passing larger estates, until I came to an unpaved road. The sound of water drew me to it and I found a creek running alongside my path. The homes gave way to woods and I felt like I could walk forever. It was a relief to be exactly where I felt I ought to be. The people were friendly, the atmosphere was light; it was a town of bakeries and bookstores where tourists and townies got along well. Finally, I turned around, not wanting to be late to class.

Pam Houston had music and props for her lecture and she out-classed everyone there with her entertaining presentation. As she gyrated in front of the lecture hall, a big silly propeller cinched to her waist and The Commitments' *Tenderness* on the boom box, I had to laugh along with everyone else in the room. She made her point about the importance of timing and style like no other writing instructor I had ever come across.

My screenwriting classes held me in good stead and I was comfortable offering my feedback on the other writers' works I critiqued. It was enormously gratifying to work and be around others who were serious about their craft. During a break between classes I asked Pam Houston to sign her book of short stories, *Cowboys are My Weakness.* Each story hinged on a great-girl-falls-for-wrong-guy premise and I enjoyed her brand of humor. Though she had written fiction, her writing was so personal and taut it inspired and intimidated me all at once. I told her a little bit about my memoir before asking her to sign her book to Bobby. I figured all my books would end up in his library one day. "To Bobby," it said. "Take good care of your Mom."

David Shields, my class mentor, passed out a schedule for the week and I learned that my piece was scheduled for critique on the second to last day. There was a great deal of material to read, daily lectures to attend and nightly readings at the local vineyards, so to begin with, I was not too focused on my own work.

However, the night before *my turn,* I began to question every word I had written. *Would anyone actually care about this topic? Did the writing hold up? Would people run screaming from the room in horror?* A couple of glasses of wine at dinner helped dispel my worries. Unfortunately, the next morning I was worked up even worse than the night before. I was baring my soul to complete strangers. I drank some coffee and blew off the morning lecture, which I knew I wouldn't be able to concentrate on anyhow. Instead, I followed the map to the next town ten miles up the road, Calistoga, and like one of the characters in Pam Houston's stories, found myself falling for a cowboy.

Main Street in Calistoga was slightly more built up than downtown St. Helena. Nibbling on a scone, I began to relax. I wandered into a few galleries. Much of the work was of the surrounding areas, of serene landscapes, of wine country in their golden green colors. Still life oil paintings of grapes and flowers were mounted tastefully on the walls. Out of nowhere, *The Cowboy* took my breath away.

It was a 3x4 foot, black and white mixed media painting. My eyes kept scanning the picture for details the way your hand glides over a present, weighing it, slipping fingers through ribbons and wrapping, each movement a visceral pleasure. In the background, longhorn cattle moved in the brush, and in foreground, a working cowboy directed them. What was so mysterious and compelling about the piece is that you never saw the cowboy's face. The artist had painted and sketched the man from behind and the rolled up shirtsleeves, the muscled arms and broad back told the story. The man sat tall in the saddle, one hand raised, guiding the round up, signaling to someone the viewer cannot see. The horse's rump and back legs are tensed, awaiting the next cue from his rider.

"The artist is Chairman of the Art Department at the local college."

I spun around, unaware the manager of the gallery was standing beside me.

"It's really beautiful. How much is it?"

"Two thousand."

I thanked him and left in a hurry knowing I had to get back to my writing class. *The Cowboy* lingered in the back of my mind, though. Its theme echoed the days of my childhood Saturdays spent on horseback with my Dad up in Griffith Park. He rode an old paint named Maggie and I was on Belle, a buckskin mare. We always sang old campfire songs. *My paddle clear and bright, flashing like silver. Quick as the wild goose flies. Dip, dip, and sway. Dip, dip and sway.* We rode for hours, sometimes ending up on the trail known as Mount Hollywood, which took us all the way to the famous Hollywood sign.

It was five years after the Napa Valley Writers Conference when I took up my search and found the painting and the artist, Tom Turner, who painted it.

"Not for sale," Turner told me. "I've gotten kind of attached to it. The inspiration was a ranch in Costa Rica where I spent my childhood summers. I have some other pieces you might be interested in."

"I have no doubt I would really like your other work, but the fact is this is the one I haven't been able to forget. Is there any way, any way at all, you would reconsider? If I'd been in the right frame of mind at the time of the conference, I would have bought it then and there."

There was a brief pause. "Well, my daughter's getting married this summer and I could use a few extra bucks."

The day I first saw *The Cowboy* I was not looking to buy anything, I was looking for diversion from the upcoming moment of critique. My thoughts quickly turned to the evaluation at hand as I drove down the highway and returned to St. Helena. This time, I barely noticed the vineyards flashing by, broken up now and then by gated estates with driveways so long, you couldn't see the home from the road. It was getting late and I had the distinct feeling I was going to throw up any second.

Finding my seat in the classroom, I sat down stiff, ready for the worst. There was a pregnant woman in class and I felt even more self-conscious about the discussion. As it just so happens, she was one of the first to raise her hand.

"I truly hope this isn't a true story, but whether or not it is, I think it's an important one to tell."

More hands came up and as comments came in, I found myself nodding my head. People cared. Their feedback was constructive but not crushing.

My instructor recommended I read Lisa Karr's Liars Club and Bernard Cooper's Maps to Anywhere. He said the material was there but I needed to find my voice. It sounded easy enough but proved to be one of the most challenging things to get straight. When class was over and I stood up from my seat I felt lighter than air; the sense of relief was like a glimpse of Nirvana.

What seemed like luxury, to leave husband and child behind, was in fact, a crucial step in repairing me. I'm convinced if I hadn't taken this time alone, I would've done something self-destructive - drink, screw around, get in a car wreck - because some days I was bigger than the emotional upheaval. And some days I wasn't.

As safe and familiar as home was, I was mired in constant reminders of what I'd lost. Going away made home feel like a brand new place when I returned. My instructor's words and the written comments from my peers gave me the confidence to keep working, and the more I worked, the more I healed.

It felt good to be back in my own bed with Neal by my side. I fell asleep quickly but a noise down the hall woke me up. I sat up in bed and saw *it*. It was short, maybe thigh-high, with a strange pointy hat and a sinister smile. I caught a glimpse of his crooked yellow teeth sneering at me before he doubled back toward Bobby's room. I threw the covers off and streaked down the hall. He was gone.

I woke up. The house was quiet. Whatever *it* was, it disappeared. As I looked at Bobby, I knew there wasn't any demon running amok in my house. I shook off the creepy feeling and went back to bed, beating back the urge to check every room and closet.

The following day I was going through my mail, when an envelope from Dr. Starre, M.D. started my heart jumping. Mistaking it for a personal letter, I quickly ripped it open and pulled out the contents. No note. Just a check in the amount of three thousand, two hundred dollars - his fee for pregnancy care. He was granting us a refund like he was balancing his moral checkbook. Still holding the check, I dialed his office number. The secretary put me on hold and I figured he'd call me later but he came right on. My voice shook with righteous indignation, like Katharine Hepburn in On Golden Pond.

"What do you mean, sending this check to me? Without any kind of note?"

"Oh, my office manager probably sent it out like that," he said. I dimly remembered his office manager happened to be his wife.

"It was cold!"

"I'm sorry."

"Listen, Dr. Starre, I understand what you were trying to do but this check came out of left field and it hurt, a lot, that you did not include a note."

"It was a misunderstanding, Cynthia. I didn't mean to upset you."

There wasn't one single moment, like the ringing of a bell, to signal my decision to leave Dr. Starre's practice. But I was so angry at the thoughtlessness behind the check being sent out cold; it solidified whatever leanings I had in that direction. It was some time before I actually sought out another doctor but deep down I knew I couldn't face seeing him again.

Neal came home from work and before he had set his briefcase down, I was waving the check back and forth in front of him like I'd discovered the missing murder weapon in a famous trial. He shrugged it off. All through dinner, I observed Neal going through the rest of the mail, checking the sports highlights on TV, and playing with Bobby. He was driving his Porsche to the office five days a week, making deals, attending meetings, drafting agreements. When you say, move on, I mean he had *moved on*. He was in fifth gear, cruising speed, while I was a stranded hitchhiker on the side of the highway, lugging baggage with my thumb in the air.

Meanwhile, I was ticked at myself for getting so wound up. I vowed to use the strength and confidence I had found in getting through the writers conference in my day-to-day life. And for a spell, that actually worked. For a spell.

CHAPTER 17:

DOUBLE TROUBLE

J ournal Entry
August 8, 2005

The problem with feeling a little better about losing Samantha is that I've been trying to do more than I'm able to. I've felt myself drowning at parties I suddenly do not want to be attending...nagging little problems with Neal have taken on more importance than perhaps they should. Music stirs me and makes me think of being someplace else, someone else...

My can-do attitude propelled me into a work mode where I started to take on my old responsibilities, one, two, three. Those duties included managing a triplex apartment building where I had lived before marrying Neal. A vacancy came up in my old upstairs unit and I pounced on getting it rented.

Clipboard in hand, I took notes with the plumber on replacing sink fixtures and with the hardwood specialist on sanding and refinishing the floor. My hands sifted through carpet samples, gauging their quality and texture. The painter and I flipped through a palette of colors as we walked through all the rooms of the apartment. Working the spike of the "For Rent" sign back and forth into the grass lawn, I awarded myself First Place in the "Moving On" award. I scheduled appointments and met with prospective tenants. Soon I was signing a lease and collecting rent. From all appearances, I certainly was getting a lot done.

The inspiration to write quietly edged away and I set the book aside. With the days of summer coming to an end, Bobby and I drove down Beverly Drive to Color Me Mine and painted purple and green ceramic dinosaurs. In between coats of paint, we would duck next door to the Coffee Bean and drink sweet, frosty Vanilla Blendeds.

Just about every afternoon, kids would come by to swim in the pool. I kept close watch over them, wrapping them in thick pool towels and offering fruit Popsicles while they dried off in the sun.

Good friends of my parents had a son Fred, who I'd seen from time to time but only known peripherally. Fred was a couple of years my senior and he and his family had recently moved to the neighborhood. When he began stopping by weekly, I chalked it up to his wanting a new playmate for his boy who was roughly Bobby's age. One afternoon Bobby and his son shot hoops while Fred and I sat in the shade of an oversized patio umbrella.

"Why aren't you sending Bobby to a private school? You guys can afford it."

"Do I tell you where to send your kids?"

"By the time he hits middle school, he'll be so outnumbered by the Persians, you'll be sending out an SOS to the private schools from Curtis to Crossroads for applications."

"What you seem to forget, Fred, is that I don't have a problem with Persians and they don't have a problem with me. Or Bobby.

Besides, how can you get a sense of community by sending your son over the hill to school?"

"Let's make a bet. If Bobby matriculates from public school at Hawthorne, I owe you one dollar. If not, you owe me a buck. Deal?"

"Deal."

"So? Where's that hubby of yours?"

"Working, of course. Where's Mara?"

"Anyone's guess."

The small talk and flirty undercurrent annoyed me. Using a slip and slide toy as my excuse, I got up to help the boys set up a game. I turned up the volume on the boom box we kept on the patio as the soundtrack to Space Jam played.

The following morning the radio was on Neal's station - sports radio with Jim Rome. Neal studied his face in the mirror, making fine adjustments to the beard he'd grown since Samantha died. Back and forth he'd crane his head, checking one side and then the other. "Is it even?"

I'd study his face. "Yes."

Peering more closely into the mirror, he had a keen look of dissatisfaction on his mug. Once again, he began to trim, trim, trim. "Keep it up and pretty soon there won't be a beard," I cracked.

He stuck his tongue out at me and made a face.

"Now there's a look."

I laced up my New Balance trail shoes and stretched my calves out against the counter of the sink. Neal turned off the radio and I looked up at him.

"What do you think about going out with another couple?" he asked.

"Out-out you mean?"

"It's been awhile."

"Okay." I kneeled on the carpet to do a few push ups.

"Are you up for it?" Neal followed me out to the bedroom.

"How bad could it be?" I said breathing harder.

He smiled at me, white specks of shaving cream still clinging to his face.

One week later we were on our way to pick up Mara and Fred for dinner at Brentwood Country Club. As I got into the passenger front seat, Fred said, "I like you out of maternity clothes."

"Don't pay attention to him," Mara said. "He doesn't know how to talk."

"Really? He doesn't?" Fred said.

She gave him a practiced, icy stare and turned back to me.

"Do you guys play much golf at Brentwood?"

"Not really," I said. "It's hard leaving Bobby for four plus hours."

"So you're really over it?" She asked from the backseat. I turned around to face her, confused.

"Over what?"

"The mourning, I mean."

I cleared my throat. "No. I'm not over it. You don't get over losing your child."

If she took offense to my tone, she didn't show it. "I just meant because you're going out and all that."

My hackles spiked like a pit bull; I was poised to pounce on Mara's neck, to seize down until I drew blood. Something soft on my hand called my attention and I realized it was Neal giving my hand a squeeze.

Staring out the window at the trees along Beverly Park on Santa Monica Boulevard, I wished like hell I was back home. The wide, dirt path running parallel to the road was filled with runners and people walking their dogs or pushing strollers. In the 1920's it served as a bridle path connecting equestrian trails along Sunset and further north to the Santa Monica Mountains where I hiked. Neal braked at the intersection of Wilshire and Santa Monica Boulevards where an old fountain stood; a Native American perched on top in a reverent pose. Colored lights blinked on and off in sequence.

Seeing the old landmarks made the voices in the car fade to a distant murmur and I started thinking about one of my heroes, Maria Rita Valdez. Around 1831, the Governor of California deeded her the land, which is now Beverly Hills. She called it Rancho Rodeo de las Aguas. The adversity of losing a husband, raising eight children, surviving Indian raids, dealing with greedy relatives and crooked politicians didn't impede her progress. My adversaries for the night - insensitive neighbors - seemed pretty mild in comparison. And after all, I reminded myself, I'd invited them out, not the other way around.

The east wall of the dining room was one long series of plate glass windows where we could look out on the dusky light as it surrendered to the darker hues of night over the golf course. Five years earlier, we'd had our wedding photos taken out there, Neal in his new tuxedo and me in a wedding gown. The bride and groom I conjured from memory felt like strangers. I smiled at Neal. We were together. We respected each other. We loved each other. Yet, I knew nothing was a given anymore.

"Life is a series of concessions and accommodations," my Dad once told me.

"Real romantic, Dad. You and Mom are a true inspiration," I responded. Okay, so when you've been married for thirty, forty years, maybe that's what it's like, I figured. Yet, here we were, out to dinner with another couple, going through the motions of being a couple and we'd only been married five years. When we got home, we would kiss goodnight, turn away from each other and fall asleep.

The waiter poured wine for all of us.

"To your book." Fred raised his glass.

I reluctantly raised mine, knowing full well he would be in it. Neal clinked his glass against mine and we each took a sip.

"Do you mind if I ask you how it happened?" Mara asked.

My sip segued into a gulp. *Oh, come on! Fred must've told you already! Don't you two talk?*

Neal took my visual cue, gulping wine, as a suggestion to talk for me. He went over what happened with the briefest of details. Mara's eyes turned moist and she swept a starched napkin across her face, smudging her mascara.

I reached across the table and filled my wine glass - the only one that already needed filling.

"Who was your doctor?" Fred asked.

"Dr. Starre."

An evil gleam glowed in Fred's eye. Mara shook her head.

"Years ago when he first started his practice he seduced a woman. A patient."

"Fred, don't," Mara said.

"Jesus."

"She came to me as a client and claimed Dr. Starre had told her he'd never seen a --."

Mara cut him off. "Fred!"

Fred smiled. "Never seen a body like hers."

By this time, the wine glass and my lips had become best friends.

Neal rolled his eyes. "Are you serious?"

"It was so special; apparently, it required further, ahem, examination. His fascination didn't last, though, and Starre changed his mind." Fred didn't register the look of bored resignation on Mara's face as he continued. "When he dropped her, she came to me and sued him for the break-up of her marriage. And he paid, boy. No questions asked."

"Whoa," Neal said.

I set my glass down too hard and if anything had actually been in it, there would've been a spill.

"Listen, Fred," I said in a low voice, "This is not something I --."
He cut me off.

"It gets better. The husband wanted to sue Dr. Starre, too! I advised him against it."

I started to object when the waiter returned with a rolling cart and proceeded to mix our Caesar salads. When he finally rolled away, I spoke up.

"Fred. Let me be really clear. I don't want to hear another word about Dr. Starre. In fact, the reason we are out this evening - with you guys in particular - is because we don't know each other real well and we were hoping to not have to visit any of this." I was gripping my napkin like a vice.

"Understood," Fred said.

Mara drained half her glass of wine and smiled at me. "It's ironic, you know. Fred and I separated recently. We accepted your dinner invitation because we didn't want to deal with our troubles, either."

I nodded and looked at Neal for a reaction. Savvy man, he wanted no part of this, and he kept to the business of eating his salad.

CHAPTER 18:

GAMBLING ON US

L abor Day September 1995

Hi Samantha,

    It's good to be here, sweetheart, among the pines and fresh air and cold Lake Tahoe. I can't get enough of crisp, clean air in my lungs. As I look around the blue lake I can't help asking myself: Why can't you be here? I sound like an idiot when I keep asking the same questions. I look for you in the reflection of the sunlight on the ripples of the lake, in the gurgle of a brook, in the fragility of a pinecone, in the smoothness of beach glass. I do have this strange sensation at times that you're close, that even though I can't see you, you can see me.

Love, Mom

The last weekend of summer before Bobby's pre-school started, we decided to go out of town. On a whim, we booked a trip to Lake Tahoe on the California/Nevada border in a little modest condominium. It had its own private beach and we played in the sand and sucked in our breaths as we swam in the chilly water. Bobby chased birds with his water pistol while we cheered him on. Then he used breadcrumbs to entice them back.

I brought my Pentax 35mm and we shot pictures of each other with Bobby. In one, I'm holding him in my arms on the sand. In another, Neal has him suspended upside-down and you can see Bobby's dimples framing his wide smile.

The towering red pines and black pines shaded the roads and paths around the lake, their green dimness making you think it was later in the day than it really was. My rental bike wheels made a pleasing crunch as they pressed pine needles into the earth. I knew better than to trust the good feeling too much - sad feelings crept up on me at the most unexpected times - but I pedaled faster and faster, feeling high on the speed.

The condo we were renting was on the Nevada side of the border where gambling was legal. Across the street from the condominium complex was a Hilton with a casino. In happier times, Neal and I had gone to Vegas to gamble, see a show and have a romantic weekend away. This time, Neal played blackjack but I found the whole business tedious. I wandered to the roulette wheel and picked "5" and "10", the month and day that were branded in my mind. The dealer handed me a stack of chips when the wheel stopped and Neal almost flipped over backwards.

"I don't believe it! How'd you pick those numbers?"

I shrugged my shoulders. The numbers five and ten were everywhere I turned. My watch. The timer on the toaster. The address across the street.

"You look pretty," Neal said.

I beamed. "What is it? My hair? The outfit?"

"You just look pretty."

"Glad it's working for ya."

He let go of my hand and put his arm around my waist instead, so that we walked side by side, almost tripping over each other's inside foot.

"Do you think about Samantha everyday?" I asked.

"Not like before." He paused. "Do you?"

"Yes."

I looked up at him for a moment and we continued walking side by side. Our perspectives would never be the same. And it didn't matter. I fell in love even more deeply with him, in fact.

Early the next morning, I snuck off to the hotel again, this time for hot coffee in a couple of to-go cups. In my haste to sneak out of the condo before Neal and Bobby woke up, I forgot my key to the condo's front gate and ended up locking myself out. There were a few options to getting back inside; I could wait until someone walked in or out of the complex or I could ring the buzzer to our unit. The coffee would go cold while I bided my time for someone to arrive. Ringing the buzzer would be a cruel awakening for Neal and Bobby, altogether defeating the purpose of my venture. That left me only one real choice - to scale the six-foot fence. The Styrofoam cups bent easily as I urged them through the bars of the gate and placed them on the ground on the other side. Then I hoisted myself up and swung a leg over the bars like I was mounting a horse. In my momentum, as I brought my other leg over, I believed myself to have truly cleared those bars - until I felt a tug and heard the rip of my canvas shorts snagged on one of the pointy tips of the gate. When I hit the ground on the opposite side and straightened up, I saw a crooked tear from the bottom of one pant leg, up to my hip. "Whoops!"

When I looked up, there was Neal. From his expression, it was clear he caught the entire bonehead move.

"Oh, good! Free coffee. Those your new shorts?"

"I didn't like them that much."

My high-pitched hee-hees and Neal's low pitched ha-has, were like musical notes winding around each other. Without thinking, I kissed Neal right there. When I drew back and looked into his eyes, I knew that whatever happened between us, I'd never find a better man. The rest of the day, whether we were on bikes, eating lunch on the deck, or playing with Bobby on the beach, I kept staring at Neal, drawn to him, like I was seeing him for the first time.

CHAPTER 19:

HORSES AND GUN PLAY

The school year began right after Labor Day weekend and we sent Bobby, now two years and nine months old, to school for the first time. Neal was excited for Bobby, who could be very shy with new people. "You're going to make so many new friends!" he told Bobby.

I was more hesitant. Sure, I wanted more time to write but it was hard to let go of Bobby and let someone else look after him. We were so close; I knew what he needed before he said a word.

The classroom was new, bright and colorful. The first week I sat on a tiny chair, along with the other moms, off to the side of the room. By the end of the week, most of the moms had left, too tired, bored or busy to hang out. Their kids would cry and wail but when they saw their moms had disappeared, they would eventually stop crying and mope around trying to make the best of it. I stuck around and many children would come to me to play with them or help them open their lunch boxes or bring down a puzzle or toy.

Sonya, one of the other moms, had a baby girl in her arms. We were sitting side by side in the tiny chairs meant for the children. She saw me cringe as the teacher came up to me and tried to politely shoo me out to the hallway.

"It's okay. I'll wait another week or two…as long as it takes for him to feel comfortable on his own," I told the teacher. When the teacher left, Sonya turned to me.

"Why don't you let him cry? It won't kill him."

Her choice of words startled me, even though she didn't mean anything. "I'm sure you're trying to be helpful, but the timing's not really good for me to have my son upset."

She pressed on, "It's good for them to get used to your being gone."

I stared at her, offended. "Look. My family and I have had tears up to here!" My hand held up to my neck like it might strike out at any moment.

She backed off. "I'm sorry."

She seemed sincere enough. "It's just that…we had a tragedy a few months ago…we lost a child."

She patted my hand, reassuringly. "I apologize," she said. "Your son and my son seem to be getting along well. Maybe they could have a play-date sometime?"

Her son became Bobby's best friend and a few weeks later Bobby was going to school, no tears, and my mornings were free to write again. Having finished a draft of the book about Samantha, I decided to take a break from it.

Other research I was poking around with led me to a true life story that had me hooked and I called Pete, my friend, and a fellow writer and producer whom I'd known since film school at USC. Pete was a tall, athletic man with a deep laugh I adored. From our work together in the past, I knew he liked period pieces and this was one about a slave during the Civil War who became friends with a famous sheriff. This was a story with heaps of action, which I knew Pete would like.

"Hey Mama! How's baby Baseman?"

"Pete."

"She look like you or Neal?"

"Listen, Pete…"

"Hey! You forget to invite me to the baby naming or what?"

"Pete! Shut up for a second. There's no baby. Something happened."

"What're you talking about?"

"She died. I had a stillborn."

"Oh, Jesus. Oh my God. I am so sorry. What a jackass I am!"

After I explained the situation to him, he couldn't stop apologizing.

"God you're making this difficult. I want to pitch an idea to you. I want to work!"

"Okay. I'm listening."

"It takes place on the eve of the Civil War. There's a traditional love story but it's almost like a love story between these two guys who don't trust each other at first." I filled out the rest of the story and waited for a response.

He didn't say anything.

"What do you think? Do you like the idea?"

"Like it? I got goose bumps listening to you tell it."

The next morning, Pete came over and we started hashing out the idea over coffee and cookies. I thought he'd be gone in an hour or two but we were on a roll and we devoured the entire platter of cookies before it was time for me to pick up Bobby. The energy and enthusiasm Pete had for the story carried me along like a buoy on a swell and I could feel my spirits rising with the work at hand.

My end of the writing partnership included the handling of provisions. Through the Fall, I had a steady surplus of Pete's favorites, including salt bagels, Madeline cookies and fresh-brewed coffee. I always bought a pumpernickel bagel for Neal, too. He and Pete would shake hands each morning as Pete would walk into the kitchen and Neal would be walking out. I think it was a relief to Neal to see me so jazzed about a project.

Another one of my jobs in the partnership was to hash out a first draft of each scene; I always felt best suited behind the computer and typing eighty words per minute helped my cause a great deal. After the pages spewed from the computer, Pete would snatch the papers in his large hands, read the lines aloud and act them out. Oftentimes this had to be executed outdoors as Pete would roll on the grass during scripted gunfights or strode along as if he were on horseback. His sound effects made me wonder if he ought to be a foley artist, one of those people who create original sounds and noises for films, instead of a writer. Writing sessions were always, always, over too soon.

We worked up until the last minute; at pick-up time for Bobby, I would burst out the doors of my office like one of my characters blowing through saloon doors and in the process, switch out of my cowboy hat into my mommy mode. It went on like that for six months until we finished a first draft of our screenplay. Time no longer crawled by. I began to feel, if not exactly like my old self, at least like a person who I liked being.

It occurred to me that having gone through my own loss, the plight of each character in the screenplay was more immediate than ever before, their problems more daunting. Aware that my mind was sharper than it had been for months, I found a deeper perspective on the work. Besides that, Pete was just plain fun to hang out with so work felt less like a job and more like a passion.

CHAPTER 20:

THE BOOK OF LIFE

October 10, 1995

Hi Samantha,

    This feels funny to write to you tonight. Between the book about you, the letters to you and my personal journal, I have days where (understandably I think!) everything gets blurred.

    I took two weeks off to write a treatment based on some comic book characters for a production company and I didn't want to leave the book to do it.

    The High Holidays took on a different meaning this year. I listened hard. I read the passages more seriously. I tried hard to think of things I could do better – be more patient with others, be more productive, but most of all, I thought about you. I believe in God. I must. How she figured this could be for the best is not something I will ever understand. I thought about Dr. Starre. Was he thinking of us?

    Love, Mom

During services, the Rabbi at our temple said: "On Rosh Hashanah a person's fate is written. On Yom Kippur it is sealed".

Heavy words - you can almost hear James Earl Jones orating them for the most serious days of the Jewish calendar. On Yom Kippur, the Day of Atonement, Jews are expected to recognize their weaknesses from the past year and to ask forgiveness of God, of themselves and of anyone they have wronged. The prayers the Cantor and Rabbi conduct are often somber. From the age of thirteen on, Jews are expected to fast from sundown the evening before Yom Kippur (Erev) to sundown the following day. One is mandated to prepare for weeks in advance through meditation and study. How else can someone grasp the full meaning of these days and experience any kind of transformation? A ram's horn, known as a shofar, is blown in a series of short and long blasts. Some interpret this as a call for God's attention.

Little else kept mine. My fast ended at breakfast, I liked to joke with my friends. Neal and I found seats near the exit so we could skip out early from *shul* (temple). Neal was more devout, fasting every year we'd been together, and many more before that. Most of the time, I felt like a hypocrite being there.

In 1995, the year Samantha died, I kept thinking about God and the Book of Life. During these services, the Rabbi talked about how certain people were inscribed in the Book of Life and well, the rest were simply not going to make it. Their time was up. What sense did it make to bring a life forward only to snuff it out? For the first time, when we read the passages, recited the prayers, I really listened. Feeling self-conscious, I mumbled my way through the *kaddish*, the mourner's prayer, even though another rabbi at the funeral told me, according to Jewish law, I wasn't expected to grieve my child, since she'd died at less than thirty days of life.

Two months had passed since I'd talked to Dr. Starre. My anger over his sending me a refund check for the pregnancy might have been too severe. Had I been unfair expecting so much from him? Why had it been so important to me for him to be my friend? Did I think I could hold onto Samantha's memory by hanging onto the relationship with the doctor who had taken care of me while I was pregnant? The more I looked at it, the sillier it seemed. Now I wanted to forgive him, to reach out and at least make it less awkward. During services, I made up my mind to strive to be more patient, more forgiving. As soon as I got home, I left a telephone message for Dr. Starre.

The phone rang a few minutes later and I rushed to answer it, but Neal and I picked up on different phones at the same time. "Hello?" Neal and I said in stereo.

"Hi. It's Dr. Starre." His voice was more gravelly than usual; it almost sounded like he'd been crying.

"Hon?" I said. "I got it."

This was something I needed to work out between Dr. Starre and myself. As Neal hung up, the line clicked.

"Hey Dr. Starre," I said.

"L'shana tovah," he said.

"Happy New Year to you, too."

"How have you been? I was going to call but…"

The line went quiet and I held my breath. I wanted to jump through the phone and shake him by the shoulders. Talk to me! Be real!

"How did the holidays go?" he finally said.

"Well, it's going to be a year of a lot of 'firsts'."

143

"I thought a lot about you. When you're sitting in temple all day..." his voice coasted away like he'd run out of gas.

A dozen responses were poised on the tip of my tongue, ready to be fired like spitballs through the phone. Why didn't he get off his behind, if he was thinking of me, and call? Uh, oh. My brand-new resolution to be more forgiving flew the coop.

Determined to leave things neutral between us, I shifted to a nuts and bolts question about my health. "I'm still lactating a tiny bit...is that normal?"

His voice relaxed. "Very normal. That can go on for months. Of course, if it doesn't subside in another month or so, call me."

"Okay, thanks." I had no intention of calling or seeing him, for that matter. Fate had other ideas.

Later that day, Bobby suddenly came down with a nasty cold with fever and was pulling at his ear. He was prone to ear infections and the pediatrician called in a prescription for him, without our having to go to his office. A small pharmacy was located in the same medical building as Dr. Starre's office.

As I waited for the prescription, the pharmacist looked past my shoulder and said, "Hello, Doctor." Out of the corner of my eye I saw a white lab coat. Dr. Starre was the last person in the world I wanted to see. It must've been adrenaline pumping through the chambers of my heart but it felt like nitro. My head whirled around to face the "doctor".

It wasn't him.

I blew out my breath, trying to calm down, hoping the other customers milling about did not notice how flustered I really was.

In the evening, Neal and I stood in the kitchen, sipping hot tea. Neal struck a match and lit a short, glass-encased yahrzeit (memorial) candle for Samantha and for his father, Robert. Little footsteps came down the hallway. Little Bobby footsteps. He still wasn't feeling well. We were waiting for him with smiles by the time he padded sleepily into the kitchen. Neal lifted him beneath the arms and held him against his chest. Bobby set his face down on Neal's shoulder. Seeing the candle, he perked up and started singing "Happy Birthday."

A little later, Neal and I kissed goodnight and I fell into a deep sleep. It happened too fast and it was not a serene sleep. I peeled back the covers and registered that the entire house was sliding beneath me right off its foundation. It was like the rolling sensation of a mild earthquake, not jarring really, but the house steadily gained momentum and a look out my bedroom window confirmed that the house was skidding south down Foothill Road, toward Santa Monica Boulevard. My instinct was to slam my foot down as if there were a brake and I could steer the house back on course, and park it where it belonged. My foot pressed down and having found no purchase, woke me up for real. Wiping the sleep from my eyes, I was still overcome with the feeling I might slide away any minute.

The following day I shared the dream with Neal.

"How do you remember your dreams so clearly?" he asked.

"It's not like I always do," I said. "Don't you ever remember yours?"

"Only the ones where I'm being chased down and someone's about to kill me."

"Great," I shook my head.

I was finally able to shake the willies while Bobby and I knelt on the floor and set up elaborate tracks and tunnels of the Thomas the Tank Engine Train set. Master of sound effects and cartoon voices, Bobby made me giggle as he became Thomas, James, Gordon and Diesel.

"OH, NOOO," he yelled, liking nothing better than to line up a series of a dozen or more trains and poise them on a ramp. He clapped as they slid down, piling into one another, crashing sideways as they slid off the track.

CHAPTER 21:

<u>DRIVERS EDUCATION</u>

*J*ournal Entry
November 10, 1995

Sweet Samantha,

Neal's in New York looking after his Mom – she's having surgery. I pray to God it goes smoothly. Praying used to be something I did unconsciously, like holding my breath when something was going wrong. Now I'm talking to God like she can hear me, like she's close enough to grasp my shoulder.

Today you would've been six months old. I look at Bobby, he'll be three next month, and know he would've looked after you like my big brother looks after me. Seeing as things turned out, it's likely you'll be the one looking over his shoulder and keeping him from harm's way, my angel.

I'm having more good days than bad ones and I'm thankful for being able to take the time to walk and hike and now I've been riding my bike, too. Being outdoors is a magic salve.

My rough draft is almost done and I'm happy about that. The last few chapters have been very difficult to get down on paper. Annie says I'm coming along and I guess she must be right because I've been giving some thought to having another baby.

I love you. Mom

The thought of getting pregnant tempted and terrified me and it was doing very little by way of bed relations. Whoever coined the cliché that sex is like riding a bike, spent more time pedaling than getting laid. When I saw the bed I thought: sleep. When I saw my diaphragm I thought: headache. When Neal came home with a box of Trojans I thought: USC.

On our anniversary, we shared a bottle of Chianti and I climbed into bed and stretched out on my belly. Within easy reach on the nightstand was the compact square package with the round ridge of the rubber visible through the clear plastic. Neal gave me a back rub and when I turned over to face him he was gentle, gentler than I wanted him to be. I tried to stir him, tracing his lips with my tongue, reaching down to the soft hair below his navel. His breathing grew deeper and faster and he started to grope my backside. We had some momentum and Neal reached for the rubber on the nightstand. He swore under his breath as he fumbled to unwrap it and when he unrolled it, the two of us were too nervous to figure out whether or not it was inside out. By the time we got it straightened out, Neal was back to square one, so to speak. We collapsed into the sheets, laughing.

My diaphragm needed to be re-fitted as is the case whenever you've been pregnant and given birth. Mom encouraged me to find another gynecologist. In a moment of fleeting courage, which isn't really any kind of courage at all, I scheduled a consultation with a gynecologist in Century City whom my cousin recommended.

Seated in the waiting room I fidgeted, flipping through my book, checking my watch, unable to concentrate on anything. *Was I going to have to re-tell the story of losing the baby? Of course the doctor would ask, wouldn't he? Was I ready to talk about being pregnant again? I hadn't talked to Neal about it, so maybe I really wasn't.*

My blouse clung to my lower back and underarms. Alternating between sips of bottled water and deep breaths, I failed to calm down. Once I sat down in the doctor's office with the view over Olympic Boulevard and the tall condominiums across the street, I got even more lost. Though I should've been interviewing him, it ended up the other way around. Breathless and choked on emotion, I re-hashed the story. When I got to "and there was no heartbeat on the fetal monitor" I might as well have been talking to a sofa. His most demonstrative response was to adjust his glasses on his nose.

Outside in the sunshine I shivered a bit, shaking off the anxiety I'd felt inside the doctor's office. I opened the door to my Jeep and quickly pulled into traffic.

While at a red light, I inexplicably took my foot off the brake and pressed the ball of my foot firmly on the gas pedal. My Jeep surged forward - a whole four feet -and smacked into the compact ahead of me. My body jolted forward, my front license plate careened into the gutter and the other driver, a Persian woman, stormed out of her car and shook her fists at me.

"Why did you do that?" she shrieked in a high-pitched voice.

"I'm really sorry." I sat motionless in the driver's seat.

"Why?" she demanded.

I reached over and pulled out my insurance information for her. The light changed and traffic moved around us. She took the paper without looking at it. With her other hand, she rubbed the back of her neck.

"Are you okay? Are you hurt?" I asked.

"Why did you do that?"

"No reason. Just a stupid mistake."

My insurance premium spiked, of course, and my sex drive plunged.

"Cindy, you've got to get another doctor. For your health," my Mom argued.

"For my health! Might as well call in a sig-alert every time I pull onto the road for a visit with the gynecologist."

"Why don't you call Dr. Fraiche? People rave about her."

When I called Dr. Fraiche's office, to my great satisfaction, her staff informed me she wasn't taking on any new patients.

"Sorry, Mom. Guess I'll have to go doc shopping somewhere else."

"Call them back. Tell them *why* you're changing doctors."

"Mom."

"That's right. You call them right now. I'm not leaving the house until you do!"

"You're impossible."

"Hurry up. I've got things to do."

Dr. Fraiche's office was different from any other doctor's office I'd seen. There were the usual diplomas, awards and textbooks around.

But there were countless hand-written letters from grateful patients all over the walls.

One of the nurses showed me into her office. She stood up from her desk and shook my hand. She was about my height, with warm, brown eyes that shone with intelligence. Her posture was slightly hunched but she had a youthful demeanor. Her long gray hair was secured in a loose bun. Dr. Fraiche listened to what I said. When I'd finished she looked me in the eye. "Poor baby."

Her face was so animated and so friendly I couldn't possibly take offense. Most people were so full of pity for me and she was really about getting me to the next step. I found myself smiling.

"If you are going to get pregnant again, you'll be treated as a High Risk Pregnancy."

I bristled at the label High Risk. "But there wasn't anything wrong with me or the baby. It was an accident."

"Doesn't matter. When a baby dies, you're automatically high risk. By the way, I'd like to see the autopsy."

"Okay."

"Not that you and Neal would have any idea about it, but Dr. Starre is on probation at Westside Regional Hospital. He has to have another physician with him whenever he's delivering a baby."

I was shocked to hear this and amazed she would confide in me.

"Why?"

"He delivered a baby with some serious problems and word on the street is he should've known about it earlier."

My head hurt when I left Dr. Fraiche's office and it was still aching after two Excedrin extra-strength when Neal got home hours later.

"Cyn, don't you remember my colleague from the office who told us that her sister lost twins under his care?"

"Come on, we've talked about all this. Every doctor, no matter how good they are, has bad stuff happen."

"Still, I want to talk to a lawyer about it. The statute of limitations kicks in pretty soon."

Neal never questioned my approach to handling my grief; writing letters to our dead daughter, wandering the beach, attending a Writers Conference, writing with Pete. If there was a case against Dr. Starre, now was the time to investigate it with a lawyer. In three months, we would hit the one-year mark since the baby died and no longer be eligible to pursue litigation. Seeing a lawyer was not what I wanted to do, and it had nothing to do with Dr. Starre's being right or wrong. It felt to me like spending energy in the wrong place. We would be focusing on the worst part of the experience. Besides, money wouldn't make us feel any better. But I was willing to go along with whatever Neal wanted for one reason: It was vital to me that Neal knew I was there for him.

I took his slender hands in mine and placed them against my temples. He rubbed my head, trying to ease away the pain. My eyes closed.

"What good can come from it?" I asked.

Sure, I had fantasies of walking into Dr. Starre's office and shrieking at him: Why didn't you listen to me? How can you live with yourself?

Neal's hands were working their magic, easing away the throbbing in my head. I sighed. "It's not going to bring her back."

CHAPTER 22:

LOOSE ENDS

February 16, 1996

Dear Dr. Starre,

I'm sending you this letter to request a copy of my records please be sent to me at my home address within the next week, if possible. After much thought, I've decided to seek the care of another physician. Simply put, I have too many mixed emotions over what has happened and as a result, I cannot continue on as your patient.

Sincerely,

Cynthia Baseman

My stomach unleashed minutes before Neal picked me up to take me to the attorney's office in Century City. Dr. Faber, the attorney Neal had found for us, had been a doctor and now he was a big-ticket lawyer. He'd won some high profile cases that you could read about in the articles tastefully placed around the mahogany tables in the waiting room. Again my Dad's words: "Marriage is a series of concessions and accommodations." In my nervousness, I reminded myself over and over that this was important to Neal and therefore worthwhile.

My husband wasn't the only one gunning for this; many friends had been tiptoeing around the lawyer issue from the get-go. They justified that in no way could Neal and I be blamed for Samantha's death, thus it had to be someone's fault. In their view, the someone plainly had to be Dr. Starre. To this day, I never could see any justice in it nor could I allow an outsider to tell me who was responsible for our loss and how much that mistake should cost.

A secretary escorted us into Dr. Faber's office. There was a sheen of cleanliness from the surface of the desk to the surface of his face. I detected the faint smell of cologne. When he rose to shake my hand he left behind traces of the manufactured scent. He got to the point quickly. "I've read through the materials you have provided. The state of California will award one hundred fifty thousand dollars as a maximum limit on settlements for malpractice resulting in a stillbirth."

Neal wore his expression bland and unfathomable as a cinder block wall.

Dr. Faber flipped through some papers on his desk. "A couple of strange items about your case. The umbilical cord wasn't included in the autopsy."

Neal and I exchanged a troubled look.

"And you told my paralegal your non-stress test lasted several minutes?"

"Maybe ten minutes," I said.

"That's a lot more time than is reflected by the small section of tape in your records. It's about a minute's worth. The rest of it has been lost...or destroyed."

Destroyed. I ground on that tidbit of information throughout the meeting like a tough piece of meat I couldn't quite swallow. My Dad had said as much to me when he'd read the autopsy.

"Dr. Starre's going to document in your chart his version of what happened. He's going to cover his back," my Dad had said.

"Depositions are often grueling. You'll be forced to relive painful moments for weeks, perhaps months. There's no way to know how long. However, if you're suffering from other symptoms…" He paused dramatically. "There may be other avenues to pursue." He waited for me to say something. "For instance, if you're suffering from emotional problems or other mental hardship…"

I ended his fishing expedition right there. "No more than anyone else in my shoes."

"Cynthia's been working on a book about what happened."

Faber's eyebrows rose into a wave of suspicion. "A book? What for?"

"It's just something I have to do for myself. Who knows? It might help others in the future."

"And how long is this book?"

"Around a hundred pages, so far."

He stared at me. He stared at Neal. We were a complete waste of his time.

"Understand something. In a deposition, they will use that book against you. If they choose to do so, they can grill you for thirty minutes on every single line of your hundred page book."

Later we walked down the street holding hands.

"So? We're not doing this, right?"

"Nope," he smiled, "How about some lunch?"

I sighed in relief.

CHAPTER 23:

FLYING COLORS

arch 14, 1996
Reno, Nevada

M According to the leafy branches on the trees and the college kids sucking down long necks at the Southwest Air terminal in the Reno airport, Spring had arrived. Neal and I huddled together waiting on a shuttle and trying to keep the guilt at bay. Our hunger for fun had edged into starvation. Although my days flew when I was working on the Western with Pete and playing with Bobby who could make me laugh like nobody's business, things in my marriage were still patchy. We were committed to one another. We didn't blame each other for how things went down. But frankly, the light, goofy, loving feeling was still in hibernation.

I was a good mom. Kept a tidy house. Held the reins on the apartments I managed. Wrote as often as I could. Neal worked steadily and with intensity. His colleagues respected him. He made time for Bobby and was sweet to me. When he came home, though, I could not be sure where he wanted to be. His honor and faithfulness would refuse to admit that aloud, but after he hung up his suit jacket I could see him searching for the television clicker, searching for an escape, for a way for us to not have to talk. For my part, I made that real easy for him. Busy, busy mom. Get Bobby bathed and his teeth brushed. Read him stories. Then it was Daddy's turn to cuddle with him and read him another story. Sometimes Neal would fall asleep in Bobby's bed while I caught up on phone calls, paid bills, read Dickens or T.C. Boyle short stories.

This ski trip was an unspoken test. Leaving Bobby behind was very difficult for me. I knew him better than anyone else. Also, I knew that very bad things could happen to my family. To me. Not for a moment did I think that the horrible pain I'd felt was any kind of guarantee that more pain did not lay in waiting for me around the next bend. My Mom was the only one in the world who could convince me that Bobby would be safe. Behind my Mom's pretty face was a hawk, fierce enough to peck your eyes out if you touched a hair on my boy's head. My in-laws flew in for a visit and were happy to be the back-up babysitters. They were already preparing to spoil him and I gave them my blessing.

Our first night in Reno I woke up in tears, my heart busted all up again. I dreamt I was back in the hospital and had delivered another stillborn - a boy. He was handed to me shrink-wrapped in plastic like poultry on a market shelf. Neal held me tenderly like a child until I finally fell back asleep.

The next morning the sunlight streamed over the snowy hills, making them sparkle with glitter. We cascaded from the top of each new run like kids. We scanned the map of the mountain, planned our runs. We held hands on the lifts, drifting quietly, up and up, glancing below at dark, icy rivers, pummeling around boulders, finding their way.

Even after a hot shower back in our hotel room, I couldn't relax. "Aren't you starving?"

"Not really," Neal said.

"Oh?" I was disappointed.

"Want me to go downstairs and get you something to tide you over?"

"Yes!"

A few minutes later he presented me with a taste of heaven in a bag of Taco Bell. The tacos might as well have been steak and lobster by the way I relished them. Satisfied, I drifted off to sleep. An hour later, Neal gently kissed me and I woke up refreshed - ready for dinner number two.

We wove our way through the crowded casino past waitresses in gold goddess outfits, holding trays of cocktails. The aroma of grilled steaks filtered through my nostrils and awakened a new round of hunger. I ate every piece of lettuce in the salad, devoured an entire New York steak and made good on a potato with all the sides. Including bacon.

After I swallowed it, Neal's eyes bugged out.

"What?" I asked.

"You don't eat bacon!"

I paused a moment and shrugged.

"Guess I do now."

We were back to being us. We chased each other around the ski runs, beaned each other with snowballs and finally, had an ease in bed that had been missing. The weekend zipped by and before I knew it, we were getting on a plane heading for home. Naturally, I hoped we could carry all those good feelings back home in one piece like the little fragile music box train we'd bought for Bobby.

Home again, I felt rested and relaxed. Bobby's grandparents had been loving and totally available to entertain him. He was delighted we were home and the quiet routine of our lives hummed along. Neal was packing up for work, and I was getting coffee brewed for a work session with Pete. Neal was thumbing through his heavy, old leather briefcase, the one he'd had for twenty years.

"Why don't you use it?" Neal asked.

"Why don't you go to work?" I was expecting Pete any minute and I wanted to get into the writing frame of mind.

"Cyn."

"Don't get your hopes up, honey."

"I don't understand you."

"The kits cost thirteen bucks. Tsk, tsk. It's not like you to be wasteful."

"Come on! Before Pete gets here."

"What are the chances? Seriously. We've only made love a couple of times."

The hurt played on his face and vanished as quickly as a sandcastle is wiped out by a wave.

In our bathroom, I unwrapped the little plastic stick and placed it between my thighs as I sat on the toilet to pee. Not looking forward to having to break the news of no news, I peered down at the EPT stick. A pink dot stared right back. My body felt tingly like after you've been thrown from a horse - happy it's over but still wiping dirt off your jeans, trying to figure out whether or not you're hurt.

Bewildered, I wandered back to the den and presented the EPT stick to Neal.

"All right!" he yelled.

"How did you know?" I asked.

Neal smiled sideways at me. "The bacon."

Some folks have it easy and know exactly what they want. Like Neal, for instance. He grinned at me.

"I don't know what to say." I glanced at the EPT stick. "We weren't even trying to get pregnant."

A sly smile crossed his lips. "Weren't trying not to, either."

My happiness hovered like a hummingbird around a lemon blossom and I tried to shoo it away for fear of tipping off Pete or angering the gods of good fortune with any misplaced bravado.

CHAPTER 24:

SAILING ON WATER AS BLUE AS AIR

We waited six weeks before letting everyone know. During a dental exam, I told Greg why I was unable to have x-rays taken. We had planned to have lunch together and he was so excited to hear I was pregnant; he could barely change out of his uniform into his street clothes. He kept trying to put two legs through one pant opening. The old advice about not counting your chickens before they've hatched became my motto.

When Neal's buddies wanted to have a party, I wasn't enthusiastic. But as Neal reminded me, we were long overdue to have the guys and their wives over. Making things easy on myself, we splurged and had the dinner catered by a local Italian restaurant. Before our friends arrived, I checked my curly hair in the mirror. I wasn't too surprised to find a new crop of gray strands had found its way through my hair like weeds.

Our parties usually had some kind of theme or game, like charades or "The Dating Game". We'd made up some hilarious ones of our own like the time we played "Author" and small teams of us would choose a book from the shelf, re-write the first line of it and the rest of us would try to distinguish the real author from the partiers. Proof that most of us possess a creative gene, nine times out of ten, we all fell for the fake. I wanted the party to be low key so I just asked everyone to bring a short piece to recite. Danny had us laughing to the point of tears with a bit about kids misinformed about world events. Scott was sweet, reading a monologue from one of my scripts. I chose one of my favorite poems that I sometimes read to Bobby while he finger-painted. It made me think of Samantha. I pictured her as a free spirit sailing above us on "water as blue as air" and as she looked down from her flight I imagined her asking herself "Doesn't the sky look green today?"

SPRING MORNING by A.A. Milne

Where am I going? I don't quite know.
Down to the stream where the king-cups grow,
Up on the hill where the pine trees blow,
Anywhere, anywhere. I don't know.

Where am I going? The clouds sail by,
Little ones, baby ones, over the sky.
Where am I going? The shadows pass,
Little ones, baby ones, over the grass.

If you were a cloud, and sailed up there,
You'd sail on water as blue as air,
And you'd see me here in the fields and say:
"Doesn't the sky look green today?"
Where am I going? The high rooks call:
"It's awful fun to be born at all."
Where am I going? The ring-doves coo:
"We do have beautiful things to do."

If you were a bird, and lived on high,
You'd lean on the wind when the wind came by,
You'd say to the wind when it took you away:
"That's where I wanted to go today!"

Where am I going? I don't quite know.
What does it matter where people go?
Down to the wood where the blue-bells grow-

Anywhere, anywhere. I don't know.

The emotion crept into my voice as I finished reading A.A. Milne's poem. There was a lull and I looked around the room thinking perhaps I'd said too much.

"Pretty," said Jonathon, "reminds me of an old Beatles song."

"The way the lines repeat sounds like a lullaby. It's great," Nicole said.

The readings continued and as Nicole spoke, I snuck a look over at Neal. Something moved on the wall a few feet over his head. Neal followed my gaze and we saw a cricket plummet from the wall onto the floor. My eyebrows went up in surprise and Neal shook his head. No one else noticed the insect except for Neal and me so it became a kind of private joke. He flashed me a conspiratorial smile and I could see new wrinkles around his eyes; a world-weariness was there that hadn't been before.

We had managed to connect our tracks but the work wasn't over. The work of two people being together never ends.

CHAPTER 25:

A SOUL IN EVERY LEAF

In April, I sensed the tremors of the anniversary of Samantha's death like a faraway train bringing an unwelcome guest. Every day, the train rolled closer, the horn blared louder, and the tracks vibrated with a steady gloom I hadn't felt in months. The books I read on loss said the same thing: holidays, birthdays and anniversaries are especially difficult. There was a new life growing inside me and I wanted to protect the baby from my own distress. Don't think I didn't buy into the theory of what I felt, the baby would feel. In no way did I want this child burdened with my own demons.

Like my past two pregnancies, I was feeling good physically - no morning sickness, just an uneasiness that made being pregnant seem like an accident waiting to happen. Knowing I had seven more months to go seemed a daunting prospect.

The Santa Monica mountains had offered me solace, so I planned a hike at Tree People to mark the anniversary on May 10th with Neal, my parents, Greg and Hayley. I had seen tree plantings and other memorial rituals during my previous hikes. I arranged for a tree to be planted in Samantha's memory. A card from the Tree People organization confirmed the planting of the tree with a card that said, "For mine is an old belief, there's a soul in every leaf."

Over the past ten months I had come to associate Samantha with the ever-changing beauty that revolved through the hills of

166

Tree People. Many others visit the cemetery during such important anniversaries, but for me, the cemetery represented one of the worst days I'd ever experienced; it was a black day void of life. It was only through the connection to the natural world – at Topanga, at Tree People, in Napa, and at Lake Tahoe – that I felt a true bond to my daughter. The changes in weather, the movement of the tide, the shifting colors of the plants, the cycle of the wild flowers all signaled to me one thing: life.

Early the morning of May 10th, before joining the rest of the family for our hike, I sorted through a pretty orange and blue striped box where I keep a collection of tiny pine cones found on my walks and colored sea glass collected on my beach walks. In recent years, my nephew has tripled my collection. I also have ultrasound print-outs where you can vaguely make out Samantha's face and body and foot prints from the hospital. And finally, I have the silver-framed photo of Samantha taken by the hospital nurses. This colored cardboard box of mine is still something I keep close to my heart. I open it now and then, not with tears in my eyes, though there's always a sharp tug of longing, but with love. The love for Samantha will always be there.

A little later, my brother and Hayley picked up my folks and we met in the old, dusty parking lot of Tree People. On the south end of the lot stood old sheds and stalls which were still in use as outdoor classrooms and recycle centers. The six of us smeared sunscreen on and adjusted the brims of our hats which reminded me of one of our family vacations where we'd gear up for some happy excursion - snorkeling in the Caribbean, climbing ruins in Mexico, boarding a bus in India. The feeling was the same; we were traveling down a road and the most important thing was we were together. The air was cool as we walked down the wide path over soft earth, shaded by sycamores and live oaks. A quarter mile later, we slowly edged up the steep, rutted grade that brought us around the north face of the park.

The first curve in the trail has no shelter from the sun and we all broke into a light sweat. My Dad was already a bit winded and my Mom was very cautious, picking her way around rocks to keep her balance. My brother eyed a buxom blond blowing past us on the trail and gave her a 'come hither' look behind her back. "She'd make it into the 'Women of Tree People' calendar," he said. Hayley cuffed him on the head and I cracked up.

We paused in a shady spot at the top of a rise while Mom and Dad caught their breath. While we waited, my Mom slid her hand into her pants pocket and unfolded a small piece of paper. "I've written something for Samantha. I'm not a writer but these are words from the heart." She took a deep breath and recited her poem.

"God Mom," I said, "that was just beautiful."

"Really! I didn't know you wrote," Hayley said.

"Thank you," Neal said. "I mean, that was something."

"Can I see that?" I said. Then she shook her head 'no' and quickly slipped the paper back into her pocket. "Come on, Mom. Please let me read it."

"Uh, uh. Let's keep walking," she said.

She's my Mom so I pressed her a little more but she held fast. I repeated a couple of lines in my head in a futile effort to remember her words.

We walked another twenty minutes or so when a movement about fifteen yards up the trail caught my eye. I stopped short and gestured to my family to check out a thick rattler, looking more like a log than a snake, as it bent and curled its way slowly across the dirt. We were in awe of its mythic proportions. The snake settled in the sun like a roadblock and stretched about four and a half feet across.

"It's probably time to turn around, no?" Neal said. We weren't in any danger but no one argued the point. As I glanced back over my shoulder I saw the rattler disappear into the brush with surprising grace as if it had never been there at all. A part of me wanted to follow that snake and see where he lived and how he had managed to evade people for as long as he had. Like many things I saw when I hiked up there, it was hard not to read a larger meaning into that snake. Did his deterring us from venturing further serve as a signal to me to curtail my mourning? Did his size symbolize larger dangers awaiting us? A friend had told me many Indian tribes believe the snake symbolizes Eternal Life, renewal and re-birth through the shedding of its skin.

For once, I tried to take him at face value; he was a healthy, native critter enjoying a piece of the morning sunshine right along with the rest of us. If Samantha could see us from her perch in the sky, I think she would have liked the way we remembered her. And to be honest, I think she would have gotten a kick out of the snake.

CHAPTER 26:

SURPRISE, SURPRISE

The hurdle of the anniversary wasn't as difficult as I'd imagined; I didn't escape into sleeping in my bed, tears didn't pour from my eyes, when I slept there were no nightmares, but May held a stumbling block I didn't count on. Sixteen weeks into the pregnancy, the doctors found something wrong during an anatomical ultrasound.

An anatomical ultrasound, sometimes called a structural ultrasound, is a study performed in the same manner as a regular ultrasound only it's a much more sophisticated device than what I was used to seeing at Dr. Starre's office. Instead of a fuzzy grayish image, this ultrasound yielded color views of the baby and all its organs. Even the blood flow through the umbilical cord was visible. It showed us that my baby's kidneys were enlarged. The specialist who ran the structural ultrasounds showed me what a normal-sized kidney ought to look like and what my baby's looked like. Big difference.

"Sorry to ruin the surprise but I need to tell you the sex of the baby."

On my previous pregnancies, Neal was determined to know what the sex was of the baby. On this pregnancy, I had prevailed upon him to be patient and to wait for the surprise.

"It's a boy," the doctor said.

"Oh." It took a moment to set in. Another boy. We weren't going to be looking up girl's names in the naming books. We were going to be getting use out of Bobby's hand-me-downs. The name, 'Joelle', I'd been toying with in my mind was no longer going to be of any use to us.

"And that's pretty useful information since we see this a lot more in boys than girls. If you'd had a girl, this might have been a more complicated situation. As is, it could be a blockage or reflux."

"What does this mean?" I asked.

"For now we just monitor you. There's nothing else you can do yet."

"What is generally done about it?" Neal asked.

"Depends on what it is. Sometimes the babies outgrow it. Or else, the baby might need surgery as early as two weeks of age."

"Oh my God," I said.

I looked at Neal, stricken. What else could go wrong?

"We'll need a sample of your amniotic fluid to rule out other health issues. And you should speak with a genetic counselor. We can take care of all that today.

Baby in trouble. The baby is a boy. Big needle in belly.

"Dr. Ehrlich at UCLA is the best pediatric urologist you'll find. I'll give you his office number."

The staff interviewed us on our genetic history and came up with nothing suspicious. A nurse led me to the examining room and offered me a gown. She wiped down my belly, sterilizing it with a cold solution. The procedure itself is well known to increase the likelihood of miscarriage and I'd avoided it my past two pregnancies, despite how popular the exam had become. The specialist came in and donned a pair of latex gloves. Neal stood by my side and I acted brave even though my heart was pounding harder than a thoroughbred at the finish line.

Neal made me promise to lay low and to stay off my feet, as the nurse had instructed me when we left the doctor's office. I know he must have been terribly alarmed, but he was acting cool and collected. He had meetings at the office and he left soon thereafter.

I fished the phone number of the pediatric urologist out from my purse and gave him a call. When the secretary patched me through, I recalled the discussion I'd had with the specialist.

"I'm having a really hard time with this. I mean, surgery on a newborn?"

"Well, number one, she should not be telling you that. There are several things that could be causing the enlarged kidneys. Surgery may not be necessary."

"Really?"

"Bottom line: it's all fixable."

It's all fixable.

The confidence in his voice coupled with my faith in Dr. Fraiche and in my own judgment helped propel me through the sobering news that this pregnancy was not meant to be carefree. At my next appointment, Dr. Fraiche and I discussed the kidney problem. Over the years, she had had patients with this issue but not a lot. Still, she trusted the specialist who was seeing me and because she did, so did I. The specialist had scared the dickens out of me, though, so I was never quite as enamored with those particular appointments.

Dr. Fraiche had been seeing me as a High Risk patient because I'd had a stillborn. She saw me often, performed many tests along the way, and generally spent a lot of time during my office visits. Her cheerful demeanor never changed even though she was very serious about taking care of the baby and me. The further along in the pregnancy I was, the more Dr. Fraiche saw me. What was great about her appointments was, she saw a lot of her pregnant patients on Sundays so Neal could come along. I remember him standing beside me, staring at the ultrasound image, amazed at the sight of another boy.

Another boy. I could call Neal 'single', Bobby 'double' and the baby could be 'triple'. I couldn't wait to meet him and I set out on reading classic boy books like <u>White Fang</u>, <u>Kidnapped</u>, <u>Treasure Island</u>, <u>The Adventures of Huckleberry Finn</u> and <u>Little Lord Fauntleroy</u>. Something inside told me I was carrying a little water baby who would be at home boogie boarding, surfing or running along the shore. My energy focused inward and I drank fruit smoothies and ate lots of protein. My ardent wish was for this little fellow to be a hardy one.

Turns out, Rachel got pregnant around the same time I did and the shared experience brought us even closer. It was a tremendous achievement for her; her first child. She didn't have the hallmark signs of motherhood yet; silvery stretch marks on her hips and boobs which no longer sat up at attention. We went out to lunch and made a spectacle of ourselves, two pregnant broads strolling down the street.

"I'm scared, Rodya," she said.

"What happened to me has got zero to do with you, okay?"

"I keep thinking something's going to go wrong."

"And that's precisely why it won't."

"Am I ready for this?"

"Like you have a choice?"

"Oh, God," she laughed.

"If I got through it, you will, too."

While I kept a low profile, hunched down under fate's gaze that sought me out like lightning seeks a tall, proud tree, she was planning a very public celebration: a baby shower. As soon as I got the invitation to Rachel's baby shower, I gave her a call.

"Rachel, I'm really sorry, hon. I can't make it to the baby shower. I just don't go to these things anymore."

"Why not?" Her voice sounded tight.

"It doesn't feel right."

"But it's me."

"I know. And I'm really, really sorry. It's just that I can't start celebrating until the baby's here, okay?"

"I'm really going to miss you."

"Forgive me, Fedya."

Her cool "don't sweat it" didn't exactly convince me she'd bought my story and I blamed myself for not being clearer. In this journey of healing, I had passed 'Point Pretend'. My travels brought me to the state of 'No Bull'. Making nicey-nice when my gut and heart had ideas of their own, felt like the most disrespectful thing I could do to a friend. A few days passed before we spoke again and I guessed maybe it was my own mind trip that had me feeling guilty. She was perfectly happy.

Instead of sending Rachel a baby gift for her unborn child, I bought her a comfy, pink robe to celebrate her and this time of exquisite anticipation. This became another of my traditions: buying gifts for pregnant moms and delaying the child's gift until it's born.

Even girlfriends I've lost touch with still call to tell me if they're carrying a baby. They inform me like I'm a shaman giving them a sacred blessing. And I do.

I pray everything will work out the way it should. If someone is at the end of their term and inducing labor is even a remote possibility, I strongly encourage them. While Mother Nature healed me better than any shrink ever could, I know her to be capricious, cold and final when it suits her.

Chapter 27:

Patsy Cline and Me

August 3, 1996

Samantha, Dear,

I've been thinking of you a lot today. Maybe it's because I'm growing more anxious about the pregnancy. I'm worried about the baby's kidney – will the problem resolve itself or not? The waiting game is a kind of mental test I could do without...

You know what else? I'm twelve weeks away from my due date and I still feel like you should be with us. That if you were here you'd be walking and talking – a toddler one and a half years old by the time this baby is born, God willing.

I still see little girls and their moms and think of us. How can I not?

I turned thirty-two last week. Never imagined life with a hole cut through it. No boundaries honey.

Love, Mom

Each ultrasound we had, and we had plenty, gave us another opportunity to see the baby's kidneys inflate. And there wasn't a thing we could do but wait, watch and wonder as the months crept by. To sit around, unable to do a darn thing, was torture.

Proving himself to be a wonderful friend, Pete listened to my tales of woe and then took firm hold of me like a trainer to a colt and harnessed my focus on our story. We busted our butts to finish "Liberty", our screenplay. The first producer to read it called me for a meeting. We set up lunch at Jerry's Deli to discuss it. I wore a black baby doll maternity dress that managed not to make me resemble a hippo. Over the past five years I had been pregnant more than I had not been but I did not care terribly much about my size.

"You look good," he said.

"For someone who's pregnant, you mean?" I said.

The producer laughed.

"The writing is really good. And I like the story a lot. Do you have anything to prove it's based on a true event?"

"Sure. I'll get you a copy of the reference book where I stumbled upon some of the characters."

"Still, I don't think Westerns are very 'in' at the moment," he said.

"Wa-wa-wait," I joked, "Go back to the part where you were saying how much you liked it!"

For the next six months, the producer had an exclusive option on our work whereby he could send it around to actors and directors. Pete and I started another story. It was a science fiction piece, which kept my mind off the baby's kidneys.

Every morning after I dropped Bobby off at school, Pete met me at home and we'd go through our ritual of making fresh, strong coffee the consistency of mud and eating chocolate croissants and fresh-baked bagels. Of course, I had switched to herbal tea months earlier.

After one of our work sessions, I noticed the baby was pretty quiet. A jolt of fear coursed through me and I called Dr. Fraiche. This baby was a smooth dude, gliding from side to side, swooshing around, not jabbing and kicking the way Samantha did. Still, I could not detect much of anything. The secretary at Dr. Fraiche's office told me to come in right away. I called Neal from the waiting room and he told me to call him the second Dr. Fraiche looked at me.

My usual stop in the waiting room was abruptly over, and I was immediately ushered into an examining room. I had barely touched my rear end to the examining table when Dr. Fraiche barreled through the door. Her usual fun chatter was absent in the silent room.

"Lie back," she instructed me. She pulled her stethoscope from around her neck, and fastened it to her ears. I lay on the table, my pregnancy jeans pulled down to my hips.

"Thanks for seeing me so…," I started to say. She put her palm up, silencing me. The cold, flat disc of her stethoscope moved slowly, then settled.

Meanwhile, I had a whole conversation with myself going on: *This baby is okay. There's nothing wrong. I'm over-reacting. Oh, no. What if he's dead?* My palms went cold and clammy and I started to feel sick.

She pulled the stethoscope from her ears. "Heartbeat's there. Here, listen." She handed me the stethoscope. Still shaken, I held tight to the stethoscope and didn't want to let go. I imagined spending hours in my feather down chair, listening to the steady sound of my baby's heart, reassuring myself over and over that he was okay.

"Can you spare one of these for a couple months for me to take home?"

She looked at me long and hard. Maybe I was the first person to ask her that question. Her eyes softened but her voice was firm. "No. You'd drive yourself crazy."

The lyrics to Patsy Cline's *Crazy* filtered through my mind. "Like I'm not already."

Chapter 28:

Save the Date

October 13, 1996

Samantha,

I think of you every day. With all my worrying over this pregnancy, I think I'm probably getting hard to live with. Make me see that all will be well!

Love, Mom

Pete and I were racing against the clock, we only had a few weeks before the baby was due, and work kept me grounded. We worked day and night and Neal would feed Bobby dinner for me so our work wasn't interrupted. Out of nowhere, Pete's girlfriend got an unbelievable career offer and just like that, they packed up and promptly relocated to Virginia. We kept at it for a while, e-mailing and sending screenplays back and forth, but it really wasn't working. The distance proved too great an obstacle for us and after a few weeks attempting to send drafts back and forth, we let the project go.

Like water filling up a child's sand pit by the shore, the hole of not working with Pete was immediately filled with a rush of things that had to be finished before the baby was born. Another vacancy at the apartment building came up and I wanted to rent the unit out quickly. I dragged Bobby with me on my apartment business,

180

teaching him a little here and there, the way my Mom had taught me.

Here he was, not quite four years old, telling me: "Mom, they need new carpets in the bedroom. And look at the linoleum in the kitchen...terrible!" I found a family that wanted the place and I took my time filling out the lease. Conducting business in my maternity dress with a mind as fuzzy as a poodle, I counted and re-counted the cash the new tenants handed me, making sure I didn't make a mistake.

Dr. Fraiche insisted I have weekly fetal monitoring sessions, which were in the same office where I had my structural ultrasounds. I'd drink tall glasses of grapefruit juice before each appointment in order to get the baby active. I forced myself not to think about my baby's kidneys swelling like water balloons since the urologist said there was nothing to do, nothing at all, until the baby was born.

There were two other fetal monitoring stations in the room so I often had another mom to chat with. They had their own demons to face - no one has weekly sessions unless there's some kind of problem. In addition, Neal and I had weekly Sunday appointments to see Dr. Fraiche. She measured the baby and checked my cervix for readiness.

"Come on, the baby is big enough to induce, isn't it?" I said.

"The baby's lungs aren't ready yet," she said.

Neal insisted we spend the weekend putting the room together for the baby. If he'd left it up to me, I'd have done no planning whatsoever. We got as far as pulling angle wrenches from the toolbox and uncovering the crib and mattress that had been stored in the garage for a year and a half. I had been putting off getting the room together, buying the diapers, and washing the linens. Didn't I just do all this yesterday? I found the pink stroller pad, washed but never used.

Neal lifted it from my hands and smiled.

"Is our boy going to be a gender-bender?" I said.

Neal handled the pad tenderly and smoothed its edges out over the stroller. "Sure, let's use it."

Every day I pestered Dr. Fraiche: When? When? When?

Finally, she checked her schedule and offered us the date of November 2nd. My in-laws booked their flights from New York and word spread out to our family and friends. Having a firm date pleased me to no end; I couldn't wait to meet this baby.

At the end of October, when I only had two weeks to go before delivery, sheer panic threatened to set in. Questions plagued me: *Will the baby need surgery? Will he be in pain? What if he loses a kidney?* Pregnancy wasn't an *experience* to me, like it is for most women. It was a trial.

The strain worked its way around Neal and me like a slow noose. I loved my husband and had every confidence we would get through this but until the baby was born, we took shallow breaths, waiting for our lives to begin again.

We did our best to distract ourselves by watching baby videos of Bobby with him to remind us what having a baby around was about. Bobby was a smiley, fat Buddha. There were shots of Neal bathing Bobby. Shots of me nursing Bobby. The three of us in the old condo in the Marina. Even though it was only a few years past, the carefree look on my face looked like another me from another life.

I rubbed my belly and said, "Bobby? Can we call your brother Harrison?"

"Let's call him Barnum HeeHonks," Bobby said.

"Barnum HeeHonks!" I said.

Seeing my reaction, Bobby toned it down. "Okay. Let's call him Aunt BowBee."

"What do you like, Neal? Aunt BowBee or Harrison?"

"Tough call but I think I'd have to go with Harrison. You okay with that, little man?" Neal ruffled Bobby's hair.

"Harrison. Harrison Baseman. It's good."

"Glad that's settled," Neal said.

I crawled on the floor and gave Bobby a hug. There was video of me playing basketball with Bobby while I was pregnant with Samantha.

"Do you remember Mommy had a big belly before? When I was pregnant and you were little?"

"No."

CHAPTER 29:

LIFE BONDS

November 2, 1996

My overnight duffle was packed and Dr. Fraiche's instructions were clear: be at Westside Regional Hospital at 7am sharp. Eighteen months earlier I had been in a room not unlike the one I found myself in. This time the room was sunny and a large window was open onto the world outside. My family was around me and the feeling was festive. I even felt peaceful going into the delivery room, which had been reserved for me. The nurse who took care of me had long, painted nails in contrast to her no-nonsense attitude. Dr. Fraiche joined us, chipper as usual, with coffee for everyone but me.

The nurse instructed me on a few things. For instance, she told me: "When the anesthesiologist comes in, tell him you're feeling the pain in your butt!"

"I'm not feeling it there yet."

"Doesn't matter. You will."

I took her word for it and as the needle for the IV pitocin drip was stuck in my arm, I didn't bat an eye. Another needle, this one in my spine. Nothing hurt. Nothing scared me. I trusted Dr. Fraiche would be there for me. My part - to dilate from 4 cm to 8 cm - required patience. Patience so that my body could catch up to my screaming head: *Get this baby out of me! Just get it over with!*

If Mother Nature had had her way, I probably wouldn't have been going into labor for another week or even two. While I waited, chained to my bed and an IV stand, I chewed on ice chips and daydreamed about the baby. I turned to Neal.

"After all this time I think I've finally nailed a middle name. Wyatt," I said.

"Wyatt?"

"Yeah. It's a tough little cowboy name."

"Wyatt. More like, *Why It*, right?" he paused. "It works."

The long, tedious labor was lightened up a lot by Neal who cracked jokes about the accommodations and the no-nonsense nurse with the nine-inch nails. Every few minutes Neal touched my hand, or gave me a kiss, or a squeeze. Sometimes I'd catch him staring at the heart rate monitor, a look of concern on his face.

During the late afternoon, Dr. Fraiche came in and slid a hand beneath the blankets to check my cervix as she had done several times during the day. "Well, I think we're just about there."

With Neal to my left, the nurse to my right, and Dr. Fraiche in front, I finally got the "okay" to push. It only took one.

Harrison was with us. Astounded, I looked at Dr. Fraiche as she expertly wiped him down, checked him, and wrapped him in a blanket.

With little fuss, Dr. Fraiche handed Neal the scissors to cut the cord, and she handed me my son. I held him close to me, barely checking out the shape of his body or the features of his face. All I wanted was to hold his little seven-pound body against mine.

I didn't get to hold him nearly long enough, before the nurses were pushing to take him away.

"Don't let him out of your sight," I said.

"Of course not," Neal said. Meanwhile, Dr. Fraiche sewed up the incision from the episiotomy.

"How's my baby?" Dr. Fraiche meant me.

"I'm good. Tired but good."

My Mom stroked my hair.

"Little Hershel, I'm going to call him," she said.

"How about "Hershey" instead - sounds less rabbinical, more... chocolatey." We laughed, punch-drunk tired. I'd been at the hospital from six in the morning until after six in the evening.

My Dad, Greg and Hayley went to see Neal and the baby in the nursery. Later Greg told me that when he'd held Bobby up so he could get a better look at Harrison, he'd yelled out, "He's bald! And he has no teeth!"

No doubt, I was exhausted from labor and from the release of tension. The storm of nervous energy that had coursed through me these past months was transformed into a peacefulness brought forth by purpose. My purpose was to love this child and I saw it distinctly. It was like gazing at a Thomas Moran painting where the sun lights up the stately mountains of the Dakota badlands and dispels the shadows. This mellow, skinny baby who had been plucked out of me early was my idea of majestic.

I savored Harrison's birth by relying on the arms that supported me. Neal nurtured Bobby and me. My folks stood over Neal and I like guardian angels. My brother and Hayley kept an ever-watchful eye. Even during labor, when my contractions inexplicably ceased, it was Greg who figured out the nurses had forgotten to release the pitocin and nothing was flowing through the IV into my system. Without him, my long labor might have been quite a bit longer. The friends I had, some old and others new, helped me heal to the point where even thinking about another baby became a possibility.

The room they offered me that night was so small it barely had room for a twin bed and the baby bassinet. Neal scanned the room and gave me a sheepish look. "Would it be okay if I went home to get a few hours sleep?"

"No problem. Me and the little man will be fine."

During our first night together, I heard Harrison stirring in the clear, plastic bassinet next to me. He didn't cry out, but I tiptoed from my bed, said hello, and gently lifted him to me. We slept together all night. When I held him I didn't know where I ended and he began. I whispered a mother's secrets to him and he understood. All the worry evaporated the way a horse will raise its head in fear to gently dropping its head.

Samantha's spirit, which I can only describe as a sense of confidence, an everything-will-be-okay feeling, filled me.

Similar to my previous two pregnancies, I had a sense of what Harrison was about. As with all children, over time Harrison's universe grew; more and more of his stars shone. Neal's honesty and lack of sarcasm were part of him. And like my father, Harrison had the heart of an adventurer and could adapt well to new people and new places. His compassion and ability to articulate his insights sprang from my Mother. He had a tremendous sense of generosity from my brother. From Hayley, he learned to question things. From me, he had a great love of nature and could appreciate the gifts of the outdoors with its endless variety of mountains, rivers, and trees. Practically every animal, from horse to snake, held a fascination for him. From the beginning, other children said he smelled like birthday cake. Harrison and I have never lost the ability to understand each other's secrets and he continues to read me like no other person I've ever met. In turn, I always know what pleases him, what drives him and what frightens him, without him ever having to say a word.

"Are you going to try for a girl?" I get asked a lot when I meet new people.

"I had one. Her name was Samantha."

As my Dad said, there are many wonderful things in my life and one terrible thing. To this day, I am not over what happened. I've learned to live with it. What survived from losing Samantha is love.

I believe Samantha goes on. The brief time we spent together as I carried her in my womb gave me a glimpse into the power she held. Her energy did not disappear. It transformed. So when I look up and see the timelessness of the black pines towering above me or I feel the strength of the tide almost pull me to my knees, I know in my heart Samantha is part of it. Her life touches me, it touches Neal, and it will always permeate my family. Our love for her knows no boundaries.

Epilogue

Shortly after Harrison's third birthday, tests proved that his kidneys had cleared up on their own. From the time he was two weeks old until he was given the "all clear", we all suffered the misery of his numerous invasive tests, exposure to radiation and daily antibiotics.

The day I learned Harrison was completely healthy was one of the happiest days of my life. I remember walking with him out of the UCLA medical offices, down into Westwood Village, where I bought him a Winnie the Pooh mylar balloon large enough to be displayed in the Macy's Thanksgiving Day Parade and a chocolate glazed donut from Stan's Donuts. Words cannot convey the relief I felt as my little boy sat there beside me with sticky fingers and a contented smile.

Each year we visit Dr. Ehrlich for a renal ultrasound to check on his kidneys. As a result of the past reflux, the left one is noticeably larger than the right. The doctor tells us it will always look slightly distorted. He also tells us it is functioning well.

Printed in the United States
106576LV00003B/248/A